Lord, Make Me Whole

HEALING FROM THE INSIDE OUT

INCLUDES SCRIPTURES AND PRAYERS FOR HEALING

JOAN E. MURRAY

Book cover designed by, Woodson Creative Studio.

Joan Murray Ministries & Seeds Of Hope Worldwide Missions

26340 FM 1736

Waller, TX 77848

281-398-2501

Contents

Acknowledgement   v

Other Books by: vii

Praise For Lord, Make Me Whole   ix

Foreword   xi

Introduction   xiii

1. Healed In Spite of Doubt   1

2. God, our Healer   10

3. Moved with Love and Compassion   17

4. Delivered and Set Free   29

5. Healing a Beloved Servant   42

6. Healing that Leads to Worship   54

7. Jesus, Have Mercy on Me   71

8. From Unbelief to Believing   83

9. Rise and Be Healed   99

10. Are You My Healer?   115

11. Beloved!   129

    A Prayer for Salvation   131

Notes   133

About the Author   135

Acknowledgement

~

I thank the Lord Jesus Christ for His inspiration, leadership, and guidance in writing this book. I am always amazed by His inspiration as I write.

I thank my Board of Directors and the Joan Murray Ministries Team for their continued support, encouragement, and prayer each time I undertake another assignment to write the words the Lord gives me.

My sincere thanks to Apostle Stephen and Pastor Christiana Mathieu, Pastor Edward and First Lady Hinojosa, Pastors Lovejoy & Charity Tirivepi, Pastors Daniel and Griselda Martinez, and Michelle Flippin for their time and commitment to reading and endorse this book.

To Julia Rigos and Michelle Flippin, you have helped me make this book something that will make a difference in the lives of those who read and apply the lessons embedded on each page.

To my family and friends, thanks for your support and encouragement in writing this book.

Thanks to the supporters of Joan Murray Ministries and Seeds of Hope Worldwide Missions for your support, prayers, and help as we take the gospel around the world.

Other Books by:

JOAN E. MURRAY

~

Boldness in Christ

Broken, Yet Unstoppable

Called and Chosen for Destiny

Discovering God Vol. 1

Discovering God Vol. 2

Faith That Conquers

Flow Through Me, Lord

Freedom In The Son

Hope In Difficult Seasons

I MUST PRAY

Lord, Make Me Whole

Overcoming Loneliness and Aloneness

Reconnect

Señor, Hazme Íntegro

Show Me How to Love

Time in Life's Waiting Room

Winning In The Battles of Life

Worship, Our Deepest Need

You Can TRUST Him

Praise For Lord, Make Me Whole

HEALING FROM THE INSIDE OUT

Joan Murray reveals the astonishing depth of God's healing nature in *"Lord, Make Me Whole."* She shares Biblical and personal accounts of healing miracles that will activate your faith in God as a caring, compassionate, and merciful Healer. Along with truly unforgettable stories, Joan offers valuable principles and prayers that will help you overcome doubt and unbelief, so you can trust God to heal you in His chosen way and perfect timing. You will also realize and learn to use the authority and power God has given you to help others experience freedom from emotional bondage, physical pain, and sickness. Lord, Make Me Whole will move you to seek, embrace, and make known the healing virtue of God.

Michelle Flippin,
Author & Speaker
Houston, Texas

The content of this book, *"Lord Make Me Whole,"* is powerful and saturated with the Word of God. Joan Murray's rich explanations of scriptures from the Bible clearly communicate the revelation she has received. She provides a personal introduction to the heart of Jesus, the Healer. Joan Murray offers new insight on topics that are relevant to every reader's life. As you read this book, the Holy Spirit will reveal areas in your own life in which transformation needs to take place so you can experience wholeness in Christ Jesus. You will examine the heart, mind, and spirit that are required for a genuine, humble servant, giving new meaning to what it takes to be a vessel for God.

Being an eyewitness to the miraculous nature of God's signs and wonders, which Joan shares, will draw you into a new realm of faith. You will be filled with new knowledge and a conviction to rise up and walk in the authority that has been given to you as a child of the Almighty, Sovereign God.

Pastors Daniel and Griselda Martinez
Templo Monte De Sion Internacional
San Juan, Texas

Joan Murray has a heart to see people healed from the inside out. We have personally experienced her dedication and commitment to the ministry. Joan has been our Teaching Pastor for the last year and we have seen great spiritual healing and growth in our church. We believe this book will give you guidelines to make you whole and will be beneficial to your life.

Edwardo J. Hinojosa, Sr. Pastor
Word in Season Intl
Harlingen, Texas

Foreword

~

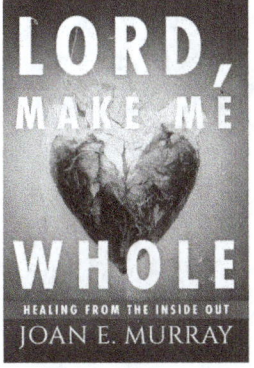

While reading the first chapter of this book, the Holy Spirit divinely downloaded to me that Pastor Joan E. Murray had a divine encounter with the God-head. I did not read sensorial theological understanding, but I read the words of someone who has been in the presence of God and has one desire: to take the people of God where she has been in Him.

The author of this book is a vessel that is totally sold out to hearing from heaven through the power of the Holy Spirit. Throughout the book, she often spoke of hearing and following the instructions of the Holy Spirit. In the first chapter, she illustrated what happened to a young boy who was sick and the subsequent events that took place in his life due to the presence and power of the Holy Spirit.

I would like to invite all the readers of this book to prepare to embark on a journey of divine encounter, led by Pastor Joan E. Murray through the words of this book. I guarantee before you finish reading this book, "Lord Make Me Whole: Healing from the Inside Out," you will experience some transformation. The knowledge of who you are as a child of God will be enhanced; your prayer life will be changed; your desire for the word of God will be increased; and your relationship with the Holy Spirit will be evident.

The following statement in the book impacted me the most: There is a higher level of authority every believer can and should operate in. At this level of authority, we can be just like Jesus in the sense that, when we speak, heaven will back us and everything on earth will line up with our request. This statement reminded me of two Scriptures from the Bible. "For from him and through him and to him are all things. To him be the glory forever! Amen." (Romans 11:36) "He will bring glory to me by taking from what is mine and making it known to you. All that belongs to the Father is mine. That is why I said the Spirit will take from what is mine and make it known to you." (John 16:14-15).

Lord Make Me Whole is for practical Christian living, because of the practical life experiences and Biblical illustrations given. The author is telling us all we know now is not all that there is to know. The Holy Spirit was given to us, so we may access all the Father and Son have for us.

Apostle Stephen Mathieu
Pastor Christiana Mathieu
Divine Encounter Glory House Ministry
Saint Lucia, Helen of the West Indies

Introduction

~

"LORD, MAKE ME WHOLE" is a cry of many people's hearts because of the tremendous struggles in their lives.

Often, we cry out to God when we are emotionally or physically wounded and need Him to step into the deep pits of our lives to rescue us. Many have experienced devastating sicknesses and diseases and run to God for peace and solace in their pain. I do not know anyone who has not experienced some type of struggle.

In the struggles, we will either run to God or walk away from Him because we may blame Him for allowing us to be in these difficult situations. We reason since He is all-powerful, He should have been able to keep us from harm. He is all-powerful, but the sin of our forefather, Adam, and some of our bad choices have caused us to be in many painful situations in which we find ourselves. The enemy is waging an outright attack against those who love and serve Jesus. God, in His faithfulness, will help us to navigate through the pain and lead us to a place of healing and freedom as we seek Him.

Life is filled with sickness and pain, and we must look to the great Physician, Jesus, for our healing. In Mark 16:15-18, Jesus commissions believers to preach the gospel to the whole world. The first thing He told us to do was to drive out the evil spirits. This is significant because we will not be able to hold on to our healing and freedom until we deal with the root of our emotional or physical problems. Our emotional wounds must also be addressed. We must dig deep to uproot the issues that have left us scarred and wounded. We must dig up each root, piece by piece, and not just deal with the symptoms of the problem. If we do not deal with the root issues, the problems will continue in our lives.

Our healing comes when we go to the only source, Jesus, to be made whole. God is moved with love and compassion when He sees us in our broken conditions. He never leaves us in the devastation in which He finds us. We must humble ourselves to receive the help Jesus sends in the way He sends it.

Because God's ways are much higher than ours, we must be open to receiving help from anyone He chooses to use to bring about our miracles. Sometimes, we may have preconceived ideas about how God will heal and deliver us. So, we may not be as receptive if the answer appears in a form with which we are unfamiliar. Naaman, the leper, almost missed his healing because he had the wrong expectations. His pride and lack of humility caused his expectations to be lofty. When God instructed Elijah to tell him to wash seven times in the Jordan River to be healed, Naaman became angry and stormed away. The answer was not what he expected, and if his servants had not intervened and challenged him about his thinking, he would have sabotaged his success.

In 3 John 1:2, the Father addresses us by telling us how beloved we are. He says, "Beloved, I wish above all things that thou mayest prosper and be in health, even as thy soul prospers." His desire is for you to prosper physically, emotionally, relationally, and financially and experience health and wholeness in all areas of life. As you read this Scripture and many others throughout His Word, you will find God's depth of love and compassion for His children and suffering humanity. The word 'beloved' means much-loved, dearly loved, adored, favorite, and darling. The Father is devoted to you, and His Son demonstrated this devotion through the cross. He is dedicated to your healing.

The word 'wish' means He wants, desires, yearns, craves, hopes, and longs for you to flourish and thrive in all you do. Your Father, His Son, and the Holy Spirit are in one accord to see that you have a rich, full life. When you are well in every area of life, you will be able to enjoy all the benefits of being a beloved son or daughter of God. I invite you to reach out and take hold of all the healing and freedom God desires to give you.

This book, *Lord, Make Me Whole,* is designed for you to remember the many healings Jesus performed on earth and remind you that He is the same yesterday, today, and forever. God sees your emotional and physical struggles and has the answers for them. As you consider the sacrifice of His Son, remember the thirty-nine stripes Jesus bore on His back were for your healing. Each time sickness tries to attack your body, remind that Jesus nailed it to the cross of Calvary, and it has no authority or power over you. Jesus paid a tremendous price for us to have victory over anything that tries to attach itself to us.

Stand in the authority you are given and walk in your healing and freedom today, in the name of Jesus!

Joan E. Murray

Healed In Spite of Doubt

A few years ago, God healed a young boy during a ministry and mission trip I conducted in Central America. After I delivered the message, I invited individuals who were sick and struggling with life's issues to come to the altar for prayer. A father came forth, carrying his son, who appeared to be approximately ten years old. The father shared the boy had missed school for a week due to sickness, but they could not figure out what was wrong with him. The young boy was so weak he could not stand on his own and leaned against his dad.

As I stepped forward to pray, the presence of the Holy Spirit was so strong the boy fell under His power. The next day while we were shopping for clothes and food for an orphanage in the middle of the busy market square on Main Street, I heard someone calling.

We approached the gentleman, and he asked if we remembered him. I told him I did not, so he reminded me he was at the Sunday evening service; I had prayed for his son, and the Holy Spirit healed him. With great joy and thankfulness, he related how sick the child had been for a week, and nothing they had done helped him, including a visit to the doctor. For the first time in a week, his son was able to return to school. As he relayed the story to us, his son, returning home from school, caught a glimpse of me. The boy ran to me and threw his arms around me, saying, "Thank you, miss. Thank you."

When I saw the joy on his face, I was so thankful the Holy Spirit chose me as the vessel through which He healed the boy. By the end of the conversation, a line of people had formed on Main Street. They asked my team and me to pray for them. Vendors who could not leave their booths asked us to stop by and pray for them, and we did. Through the power of the Holy Spirit, God healed one young boy and opened the way for us to minister, pray, and lead several people to His Son, Jesus Christ.

Although stories like this abound, many of us still struggle to believe God desires to heal us. The Bible says Jesus is the same yesterday, today, and forever (Hebrews 13:8). This means He does not change; what He did centuries ago, He is still doing today. Jesus is still healing the sick and the diseased. He is still delivering people from the traps of the enemy. He is willing and available to heal and deliver even you today.

Jesus wants us to experience wholeness in every area of our lives—our emotions, souls, and bodies. He bore thirty-nine stripes on His body so that we could be healed (Isaiah 53:4-5). He also wants you to experience healing in all areas of your life. We will explore the physical healing Jesus provides and the emotional and spiritual healing many need. God wants you to know He loves you and understands your weaknesses and diseases; He will surely do something about them.

I was introduced to the Healer, Jesus, in my early twenties. Several years ago, I was saved and had been learning the benefits of having an intimate relationship with God, including the gift of healing. I began to pray for people struggling in life, especially with sickness in their bodies. It was important to me because I had suffered from an ulcer since I was sixteen. I had been praying the Word of God over myself and believing in my healing for two years, so I was willing and available to pray for others.

One day, a lady approached me and asked for prayer. She said she had a bleeding ulcer and was slated to have surgery in two weeks. Are you surprised God brought this lady to me with the same condition I had? Do not be surprised. God never wastes anything in our lives. He uses what the enemy means for evil and turns it for our good, and often, into some of our finest moments. This lady and I prayed together, believing God would hear and answer our prayer. He did. Two weeks after we prayed and before her surgery, she asked the doctor to do another ultrasound because she was feeling much better and not having the continual pain. To the amazement of the lady and her doctor, the ulcer had begun to dry up. Since her wound was healing, she did not need surgery.

When she shared this praise report with me, I was not only amazed but also confounded. I was confused because I had been praying for healing for myself for two years and still had the ulcer; yet, God healed this woman within weeks. Although I was elated and overjoyed to know my prayers worked, I was disappointed my healing had not yet manifested. You can imagine the conversation I had with God regarding this. I naturally wanted to know why He had readily healed this lady while I had been suffering for years and taking all kinds of medicine to ease my discomfort.

In your walk of faith, God does not necessarily give you the answer you seek when you desire it. His words to me were, "I am going to heal you, and you must trust Me." He indeed healed me – ten years later.

We understand many things about God but do not always understand His timing. In my situation, He did not heal me immediately, but He instantly cured the lady for whom I had prayed. When you pray and God does not move on your behalf as you expect, remember He knows everything and is always working things in your favor. If you trust Him, you will discover His plans will far exceed what you have planned for your life. I will share later in the book about the waiting season for my healing and why God delayed it.

Our desire to be healed and whole is also the desire of God's heart for us. In 3 John 1:2, He says, "Beloved, I wish above all things that you may prosper and be in health, even as your soul prospers." He calls you His beloved, His dearly loved ones, and he desires that you have prosperity in all areas of life. In Exodus 15:26, God says He is the God who heals us. In Hebrew, "Who heals us" is a single word meaning "your Doctor." God, as our Doctor, provides our healing through the pain and suffering of His Son, Jesus Christ, on the cross.

When Jesus was on earth, He performed thirty-five recorded miracles. Please note the word *recorded* because the Bible says He did many more that were not recorded. Seventeen of the miracles Jesus performed were the healing of peoples' bodies. Nine of His miracles involved overcoming the forces of nature; six were deliverances from demonic oppression, and three miracles raised people from the dead.

In the three short years of Jesus' ministry on the earth, He showed us the heart of God concerning the well-being of His children. God wants us healed! Hebrews 4:15 says the feelings of our infirmities touch Jesus, and he is our Doctor—the Great Physician. This means He feels what we feel and suffers right along with us when we encounter pain in our bodies and anguish in our souls.

The Holy Spirit is still healing people today, and He is using believers who are willing to be the hands and feet of Jesus. He is consumed with the compassion of the Father and Son and longs for us to be made entirely well. Healing means mending, curing, repairing, easing discomfort, and restoring. Not only does God want to mend and heal, but He also wants to restore what was lost amid our suffering. As you allow this truth to settle in your heart, you will have faith to reach out and receive the healing God longs to give you.

Healing was always a part of God's divine plan of prosperity. It is hard to enjoy the blessings of God when you are not physically well. We have heard of many wealthy people who are sick and cannot enjoy their wealth. Some of these people would do about anything and pay any price to be well again. Remember, the Healer has always been with us, and He is ready to heal us each time we ask. However, like me, the healing may not be instantaneous. But if you keep the faith, He will heal you. I invite you to journey with me through the Old and New Testaments to see that God has healed throughout the centuries and will continue healing until Jesus returns for His people.

Healing a Leper

Not only did God the Father heal leprosy in the Old Testament, but His Son, Jesus, also healed many lepers in the New Testament. In 2 Kings 5, we find the story of a Syrian Commander whom God dramatically healed. His story is filled with lessons for us as we position ourselves to receive from God.

Now Naaman was commander of the army of the king of Aram. He was a great man in the sight of his master and highly regarded, because through him the Lord had given victory to Aram. He was a valiant soldier, but he had leprosy. Now bands of raiders from Aram had gone out and had taken captive a young girl from Israel, and she served Naaman's wife. She said to her mistress, "If only my master would see the prophet who is in Samaria! He would cure him of his leprosy." Naaman went to his master and told him what the

girl from Israel had said. "By all means, go," the king of Aram
replied. "I will send a letter to the king of Israel." So Naaman left,
taking with him ten talents of silver, six thousand shekels of gold
and ten sets of clothing.
2 Kings 5:1-5 (NIV)

Naaman, this beloved commander, had leprosy—a skin disease that carried a stigma. Leprosy eats away at the flesh, causing the loss of body parts (e.g., fingers, hands, nose, toes, etc.). Even though Naaman had a high and lofty position among the people, his leprosy made him an outcast in society. Because the disease was contagious, he could not get close to people. Only his high-ranking position and usefulness to the king had kept him from being put away in a leper colony. Throughout the Bible, we read stories of lepers who were often separated from their families, friends, and homes. They could not live among others because of their disease. Naaman still had access to his house and family but felt the other limitations. Not only did the condition carry a stigma, but no hope for a cure existed.

Although Naaman was a Syrian and not one of God's chosen people, he found favor with God because God used him to bring freedom to Syria. God put a strategic plan to heal him because his healing would be a testimony to many. Since he was an honorable man with a God-given assignment, God positioned around him all the right people who would help facilitate this healing miracle. God used a young servant girl from Israel, Naaman's wife, his servants, and Elisha the Prophet to perform this amazing miracle.

God will position people in your life that He can use to help you get your miracle. Can God heal you without assistance from others? Yes. He can, but He likes to involve people in His work. When God uses us, it helps open our eyes to what He is doing around us and the world.

Before connecting with Naaman, Elisha, the prophet, had just raised the Shunammite woman's son from the dead (2 Kings 4). His faith was at a high level after such a great miracle, and this was God's perfect timing for Naaman to receive his miracle. The young servant girl had set the stage by sharing her faith with Naaman's wife and introducing her to the God who heals. She shared the stories and miracles of the prophet Elisha and encouraged the wife to speak to Naaman about his healing.

After the conversation, Naaman approached his king, who gave him permission to go and seek his healing. The king of Aram sent a letter to the king of Israel requesting healing for Naaman. This request distressed the king of Israel. He thought the king of Aram was looking for a quarrel with him because he did not have the power to heal Naaman. Upon hearing about the request, Elisha told the king of Israel to send the leper to him. There was indeed a prophet and a healer who had the ears of the God of heaven and earth.

God used a slave girl to introduce His power to Naaman's family and all who knew him. As we look at this young slave girl's life, we see faithfulness in action. Although she had been taken from her home and family and served as a slave, she did not allow bitterness and unforgiveness to take root in her heart, nor did she blame God for her situation. She shared her love for Him and faith with those who needed Him. It is apparent she had an intimate relationship with the Father. She understood He had an assignment for her wherever He planted her, and she found her assignment.

God uses people who are available to Him no matter what adverse situations they may find themselves in. God is never taken by surprise when difficult circumstances arise in our lives. If He allows the difficulties, He will use them to bring about His greater plan in and through us.

God often works through people. He uses us to be His hands and feet for those who need a touch from Him. Naaman needed healing, and God used the prophet Elisha to heal him. God could have spoken the words, and the healing would have manifested, but there are many lessons to be learned when God works through us, His creation. In the upcoming chapter, I want us to look at the process of Naaman's healing. In his healing, we will see that God works through us when we are humble and allow Him to use whatever is necessary to accomplish His job.

Lessons To Live By

- Be ready and available to be used by God.
- God can use you even in the difficult seasons of life.
- Do not let your position or status in life silence your voice; you have something to say for God.
- Be bold and speak up for God.
- God can use anyone at any time if He chooses; Our circumstances do not limit him.
- If you miss an opportunity to be used by God, keep looking. He will present another opportunity.

A Scripture for Healing – Psalm 107:20

Father, thank You that Psalm 107:20 gives us a great promise. It tells us You sent Your Word and healed us. Today, I choose to take Your Word as medicine for my soul, and I thank You that as I speak it over my life, it will bring healing and wholeness to my body as well as my emotions.
In Jesus' name.
Amen!

God, our Healer

When the hand of God touches you, you will be radically changed. God is such a personal God that He will step into your life at the right time to heal the broken places, not only in your body but also in your soul. We may often feel we are in control of what happens, but when sickness attacks us, we realize we are not in control.

We need God to come to our rescue. He came to Naaman's rescue and forever changed his life and the course of his destiny. God, our Healer, causes us to experience such freedom and peace in our bodies and emotions; beyond a doubt, we will know He is the One who has worked His miracle in us. His healing power brings hope to our wounded hearts just as it did for Naaman.

Elisha asked the king of Aram to send Naaman the leper to him, but when Naaman arrived, Elisha refused to meet him face-to-face. Instead, he sent his servant to tell Naaman to go and wash seven times in the Jordan River. Naaman felt insulted and became angry that the prophet did not come out to meet with him (2 Kings 5:9-10).

When Naaman came to meet Elisha, he had great expectations

of the outcome, but his expectations were not met. He reminds me of many of us who are hoping God will move in a specific way in our lives, and when He does not move as we expect, we become offended. We often put limitations on how God can and will answer our requests. However, God has His ways and plans for the outcome He desires. God may not respond to our requests and expectations within the time limitations or the boundaries we have established for Him. Remember, He is God and is not subject to us; we are subject to Him. When He gives us instructions for our miracle, we must decide whether we will follow them or miss out on those opportunities.

Naaman almost missed his miracle because of wrong expectations and becoming offended. Naaman was given explicit directions for his healing but did not cooperate because he felt other rivers in Damascus were better and cleaner than the Jordan. He refused to wash in the Jordan River. Some of us may feel we are more knowledgeable than God, and we can miss His miracles in our lives because we do not readily receive His instructions. Naaman almost missed his divine visitation because he thought he knew what was best.

Let's look at the history of the Jordan River to see why Elisha would possibly send him there to wash and receive his healing. The Jordan River was located in Israel. The word Jordan means flowing downward or the descender. It is the river the Israelites crossed over under Joshua's leadership to get to their Promised Land, the land flowing with milk and honey. The Lord performed a miracle to stop the flooding of the Jordan River, which allowed the Israelites to cross safely (Joshua 3:16).

The Jordan River was also very special to Elisha because it was where he saw the Lord take Elijah into heaven and took Elijah's mantle, which fell and proved the Lord was with him (2 Kings 2:11-14). John the Baptist had his baptism ministry at the Jordan River. At the Jordan River, Jesus was water-baptized, and God spoke from Heaven, saying Jesus was His beloved Son in whom He was well pleased.

Many miracles had already taken place at the Jordan River. Elisha sent Naaman there to wash and be made whole, but his pride got in the way. Why was Naaman so upset at the request? I believe it was because Elisha did not meet with him in person, even though he had a high-ranking position. He probably felt dishonored and disrespected. The prophet Elisha was wise and received instructions from God concerning handling this miracle. God was after much more than Naaman's physical healing; he was after the pride that was deeply rooted in his heart. Pride has caused the downfall of many people, not just those with high-ranking positions but even those who do not have much earthly status or position. You and I must choose to be humble, obey God, and follow those He sends to help us in our crises.

The servants who traveled with Naaman witnessed his attitude and challenged him. They addressed him as "My Father." This address speaks of a more intimate/familiar relationship than slave and master. They asked him if the prophet had told him to do something greater, would he not have done it? These servants operated in great discernment and went right to the core of his problem. He felt what the prophet had asked him to do was beneath him—his rank, status, and position in life.

Their question showed they recognized his pride would cost him something precious. The healing he longed for was within his reach, but his pride and anger almost caused him to miss it.

God does not act randomly. God uses people in our lives to get us into position for the plans and purposes He has for us. Naaman was teachable and listened to the wisdom of his servants and those under his leadership, which shows he had a degree of humility. Why did Naaman listen to his servants instead of Elisha? It could be because of his relationship with them. They had served with him and been through difficult wars together, and he trusted them because he knew they were genuinely concerned about his wellbeing.

I am convinced Naaman heard about other miracles Elisha had performed, so he should have operated in greater faith, but he lacked trust and confidence in the instructions he received. I am reminded of how sometimes we also do not trust God's instructions, and we may lack the faith to believe He will heal us, especially if we have been waiting for a long time.

Sometimes, we also get angry and frustrated because the miracles we have been praying for have not yet manifested. The wait may have eroded our trust and confidence in God. As you wait for your healing, remember God is with you. Although we do not always understand His timing, He will manifest His promises in your life because it is according to His will. I can tell you I do not always understand His delays, but I have come to trust that in the delays, He is working things in our favor. I am constantly reminded that God's vision and His view of our lives are far greater than ours. He sees from a higher and greater perspective than we do, and we must trust Him. Trusting Him is deciding based on your past experiences of His faithfulness in your life. He is trustworthy; therefore, you can be assured that what He sees in your future is always far beyond what you and I can comprehend.

Naaman's Healing

Once Naaman's servants had challenged and corrected him, he obeyed Elisha's instructions and dipped seven times in the Jordan River. After the seventh dip, he came up totally healed and completely whole. In the Bible, the number seven means completion, and the number eight means a new beginning. Naaman received both a healing and a wonderful new beginning.

After being healed, Naaman returned to Elisha, and this time, Elisha came and met him face-to-face. Let us examine some of the lessons embedded in this healing and their exchange.

> *Then Naaman and his entire party went back to find the man of God. They stood before him, and Naaman said, "Now I know that there is no God in all the world except in Israel. So please accept a gift from your servant." But Elisha replied, "As surely as the Lord lives, whom I serve, I will not accept any gifts." And though Naaman urged him to take the gift, Elisha refused.*
> *2 Kings 5:15-16 (NLT)*

In Elisha's conversation with Naaman, we see the visible power of God. I contend that if Elisha had initially met Naaman and laid his hands on him, Naaman would have given credit to the prophet for his healing instead of God. Naaman would not have known God was the only Healer and that He only uses people to carry out His desires in our lives. He would have worshiped the prophet instead of the Creator. Elisha was wise and in tune with God to know God wanted absolute credit for this great miracle. Elisha also understood human nature. We tend to worship people because we cannot see God with the naked eye. Therefore, we are challenged to believe He is available to heal us. We must always look to God for our healing and not to man. Naaman, with a thankful heart, realized there was no God on all the earth but in Israel. He attempted to give gifts to the prophet in appreciation for the miracle, but Elisha would not accept them.

Naaman promised to worship and sacrifice to no other God but the one true God. His heart belonged entirely to God. In Luke 4:27, we read something very interesting. It says, "And there were many lepers in Israel in the time of the prophet Elisha, but the only one healed was Naaman, a Syrian." This scripture tells us God bypassed all the other lepers, even among His own people, the Israelites, to heal this one unbeliever. This example of God's compassion tells us He also has compassion for those who do not claim Him as Lord, and He is willing to heal and set them free.

As we serve Him, we must also reach out to those who do not readily accept the sacrifice of His Son. In doing this, we can reach others with the power of His healing touch. God will use the healings, prophesies, miracles, and deliverances as open doors to show people how powerful and available He is to those in need. He will cause them to see, just as Naaman saw, that there is no power in the entire world greater than His.

Lessons To Live By

- God uses people to bring about our miracles.
- God has an assignment for you to be a part of someone else's miracle.
- We must speak up for God when we are given the opportunity.
- It takes faith for us to operate in the healing power of God.
- We must let go of pride to receive our miracle.
- Look to God and not man for your answers and miracles.
- Do not attempt to steal the glory that only God deserves.
- Be humble, and remember, God honors those who operate in humility.
- After God uses you, do not attempt to profit from it.
- God will always bless those who obey.

A Scripture for Healing – Exodus 15:26

Father, thank You that Exodus 15:26 says if I will listen carefully to the voice of the Lord my God and do what is right in His sight, obeying His commands and keeping all His decrees, then He will not make me suffer any of the diseases He sent on the Egyptians *for He is the Lord who heals me.*
I pray this in Jesus' name.
Amen!

Moved with Love and Compassion

⟡

Throughout the New Testament, we find many instances of Jesus' love and compassion for those who were sick and diseased. He healed and delivered many people who the devil oppressed. He was not a distant Savior, and He always stepped into the broken lives around Him to bring hope and healing. Jesus was moved with compassion when He saw the people's pain, struggles, and hopelessness.

He did not turn His face away from those who were hurt and wounded. The example given to us is to be moved by love and compassion for the hurting and the oppressed. We are called to be His hands and feet in a decaying and dying world. We are expected to stop and address the conditions of hurting humanity, even when we are busy. Jesus has filled us with His Holy Spirit and power to make a difference everywhere we go. We are to impact lives in homes, neighborhoods, communities, restaurants, and stores, on the job, and around the earth.

In John 14:12, Jesus says, "I tell you the truth, anyone who believes in me will do the same works I have done, and even greater works because I am going to be with the Father." I know you are asking, "How can I do greater works than Jesus? He healed the sick, delivered the oppressed, and raised the dead—He was Jesus!" And Jesus gives us the answer: we will do more wondrous works when we believe in Him. We must believe He is the Son of God. We must consider what the Bible says about the miracles Jesus performed and emulate Him. We must understand we are not the miracle worker; He is and will do the work through us. Jesus also says greater works will we do because He is going to the Father. When He went to the Father, He gave us an incredible gift. He sent us the Holy Spirit, the One who worked alongside Him in performing these amazing miracles. The Holy Spirit is the One who gives us the gifts of the Spirit, and He will perform great miracles through us. He is our Miracle Worker.

In this chapter, I want to look at what the power of love and compassion can accomplish. In Luke 7, we find the story of one of Jesus' great miracles.

Soon afterward Jesus went with his disciples to the village of Nain, and a large crowd followed him. A funeral procession was coming out as he approached the village gate. The young man who had died was a widow's only son, and a large crowd from the village was with her. When the Lord saw her, his heart overflowed with compassion. "Don't cry!" he said. Then he walked over to the coffin and touched it, and the bearers stopped. "Young man," he said, "I tell you, get up." Then the dead boy sat up and began to talk! And Jesus gave him back to his mother.
Luke 7:11-15 (NLT)

Jesus raised three people from the dead during His earthly ministry. He raised this young man, a ruler's daughter, and Lazarus. This young man was on the way to the funeral, so he probably hadn't been dead too long. The ruler's daughter had just died when she was raised. Lazarus was dead for four days before being raised. In those days, people buried the dead as soon as possible since there were no refrigerators to keep the bodies, which would begin to stink very quickly. Jesus ministered in all stages of death, and since He also expects us to raise the dead, we can also minister in all stages of death. In raising these three people, Jesus brought resurrection life to them. He changed their circumstances by restoring joy and hope to them and their families.

Jesus was moved by compassion when He encountered the grieving mother on her way to the funeral. Since she was a widow, her primary support came from her son, who was now dead. She grieved not only the loss of her child but also the loss of her financial support.

She was a daughter of God, and He sent His Son at the right time to help her with her difficulties. Jesus was given a divine assignment to connect with her at this precise time in history, and He did not miss His assignment. He was positioned at the right place and time to meet her at the point of her greatest need.

Some of you may be wondering why He did not arrive when the man was sick and before he died. Indeed, He could have come before this young man's death, but the power of God displayed in this resurrection would not have been witnessed by the many people who saw it. The large crowd that followed Him would not have come to know Jesus was indeed the Son of God.

God's timing is beyond our understanding, and He does not function within our time frame. Isaiah 55:8-9 says, "For my thoughts are not your thoughts, neither are your ways my ways, saith the LORD. For as the heavens are higher than the earth, so are my ways higher than your ways, and my thoughts than your thoughts." This scripture shows that our thoughts and ideas cannot compare with God's thoughts and how He operates. We could say He sees from an eagle's viewpoint while we only have a bird's eye view. His view is clear and unobstructed, while ours is unclear and unfocused. It is, therefore, impossible for us to know what and when the best time is for Him to move in our situations. When He does move, it is because all the components are in place for us to either receive the miracles or be an eyewitnesses to them.

Think with me for a moment. If Jesus had arrived a day earlier, a few minutes later, or a few minutes earlier, would He have connected with the woman and her son at the right time? No. As we consider this miracle, part of the miracle was God's perfect timing for this woman and her son. Time is entirely in God's hands, and He works within His time frame to bring His work to our lives and around the world. If you and I can simply trust and rest in His faithfulness, we will never become anxious about whether we will miss His perfect timing for our lives.

In restoring this woman's son to her, Jesus takes us to the Old Testament, where we find God also restored sons to widowed mothers. In 1 King 17, God sent Elijah to connect with a widow at Zarephath because there was a famine in the land, and she and her son would have died without the provision He had for them. God knew this widow would lose her primary support if her son died, so He sent provisions through the prophet.

When Elijah found her, she was in a hopeless and desperate situation, but God still asked her to give her last meal to produce her miracle. She had to feed the prophet first with the bit of food she had left in her barrel. By faith, this widow obeyed Elijah and gave him her last meal, and God honored her with an abundant supply throughout the famine. After she obeyed and fed him, God performed the miracle of providing a bountiful harvest in her life.

God required her last bit of food because she would encounter a more significant challenge along the journey requiring absolute trust and faith in the prophet and God. Shortly after feeding the prophet, her son became ill and died. I believe the bread and oil miracle was not the greater miracle; it was the miracle of her son being raised from the dead.

The increase in her faith after the first miracle caused her to believe God could raise her son from the dead. So, when her son died, the woman did not weep and wail. She became angry. In her anger, she went to Elijah and demanded to know if he had come to bring her sins back to remembrance and to slay her son.

At times, we may think our sins are the reason we struggle and do not experience the blessings of God. Even though our sins can negatively impact our lives because there are always consequences for disobedience, sometimes the devil targets us. The devil understands human nature and uses our difficulties to divide and conquer us. He brings problems to make your life unbearable. He knows these situations will keep you from pursuing God and from staying close to Him when you need Him the most. The goal is to separate you from the One who loves you and will help you face and overcome every trial. The enemy tells you God could have changed the outcome in your favor but did not.

When he plants these seeds in our minds, they can be hard to dislodge, and after a while, we sometimes begin to blame God for not watching over us.

This widow fully expected Elijah to do something when she stormed up to him in anger and demanded an answer. She expected a miracle greater than the one she had already received. God responded by raising her son from the dead. He used the anointing on the prophet's life to perform this great miracle.

Again, we see God's perfect timing in this widow's life. God had positioned the prophet in the right place at the right time so he could raise him from the dead when the child died. After Elijah raised the child from the dead and God restored him to his mother, she said something that I found surprising. She said, "Now I know for sure that you are a man of God and that the Lord truly speaks through you." It is very apparent she did not at first believe in the prophet, even after God used him to supply her needs. Her statement speaks of her struggles and doubts in believing God would come to her rescue. When He gave her the first miracle, she received it but did not wholly believe Elijah; only after the second miracle did she fully open her heart to him and God, who had sent him into her life to help her and her son.

Some of us can see ourselves in this woman's struggle and her response to it. We sometimes lose hope during our struggles and the long seasons of waiting for God's promises to manifest in our lives. When the miracle comes, we are often unmoved because our hearts have become callused during the waiting. Sometimes when the blessings arrive, we have cried so many tears and are so down-trodden it is almost impossible to get excited about what God has done. The amazing thing about this story is God will help us and come to our rescue even when we have become cold in our emotions toward Him.

In 2 Kings 4, we see how God provided for another widow. Elijah's protégée, Elisha, encountered another widow at a desperate point in her life. Her husband had died, and the creditors were attempting to take her two sons as payment. Elisha asked her what she had in her house. She had only a pot of oil. Interestingly, with the widow from Zarephath, God used what she had in her hands to perform her miracle, and Elisha asked this second widow what she had in her hands that could help create her miracle. God will work with what you have to make a miracle in your life.

Once she told Elisha what she had, he instructed her to go and gather all the empty vessels or containers she could find. This widow had to sow into her miracle. After collecting the containers, Elisha told her to go into her house and close the door. I believe Elisha kept her from being distracted by nosey neighbors who may have questioned why she wanted all those containers and how she was expected to fill them with so little oil. Elisha was making sure there were no doubters and unbelievers who could speak negatively about the miracle God was about to perform in her life. The widow's faith and her focus had to be entirely on

God. She closed the door, poured, and kept pouring the oil until all the vessels were full. (If she had more containers, the oil would not have stopped flowing until all the containers were full.) She was then able to sell the oil and save her sons.

As you study the Bible, you will find God has always looked upon the plight of widows and orphans and has great love and compassion toward them. It may appear, Elijah and Elisha, just happened to be in the lives of these widows by luck, but that is not so. God knew them, saw their struggles, wept with them over their losses, and then decided to intervene. He strategically placed the prophets in their lives because without them, their sons would have been lost, and the widows would have experienced even more hopelessness. God showed His love and compassion toward them and did not leave them in the broken conditions in which He found them.

When contrasting the miracle of Jesus raising the widow's son in Nain with those of the prophets, we see something different. Elijah had to do something to raise the widow's child from the dead. He took the dead child, laid on him, and prayed and petitioned God earnestly, and God heard and answered. Elisha told the other widow to find something in her house to help produce her miracle. Jesus, the Son of God, had all power and authority in His hands and operated in it. Being moved with compassion, He took pity on this weeping widow and encouraged her not to weep. He walked up to the casket and spoke tender words filled with love, "Young man, I say unto thee arise." No great effort, no praying and petitioning God, no excessive work. He was moved only with love and compassion, which He poured into the heart of this helpless widow and her son to bring restoration.

I can imagine the fear and confusion of the people who witnessed this event. Many realized they were privileged to meet the universe's Savior and accepted Him as King. Others probably walked away afraid and confused. Unwilling to surrender their hearts to Him, they missed their divine visitation from God.

We can also perform miracles like Jesus did if we operate with the power and authority at our disposal. The power of the Holy Spirit that worked in Jesus' life is also available to every believer who will say yes to God. God will use you to perform great miracles as He did with Jesus, the Apostles, and many other modern-day men and women. I believe the most significant ingredients to produce miracles are love and compassion. When we tap into God's love and mercy for mankind, we will see great miracles on earth.

One incident my team and I experienced while on a mission trip left an indelible impression on our hearts. We served at an orphanage for children and teenagers who had AIDS. Those who took care of the children were caring and kind. You could see the compassion of the Lord in them as they served. The children were happy and loving. We had the privilege of sharing Christ with them, playing with them, feeding them, and clothing them. As we ministered, one of the team members noticed a little girl in a wheelchair who was extremely quiet and shy. Several other team members tried to engage her in conversations, but she was unresponsive. The Lord told this team member to ask the young girl what she would want if Jesus could give her anything. With head bowed down and in a tiny voice, she said, "A doll." The doll she wanted should have all the clothes and accessories so she could dress it and fix her hair.

Before going to this orphanage, we were told the things the children needed most, and those were the items we initially provided. Upon hearing the request of this young girl, we realized that giving the things they needed was fine, but children also needed toys and gifts to brighten their days. Armed with this knowledge, we went shopping for all the children and returned to the orphanage with many surprises. The joy and excitement on the children's faces were beautiful. The young girl looked up at us for the first time when we presented the doll. The smile that came to her face as she held tightly to her doll was priceless.

We must learn to hear God's voice and obey when He speaks to us. If we do not listen to Him, we will miss opportunities that will leave a mark on our hearts and the lives of others. We left the orphanage feeling we had become more like Jesus, being filled with His love and compassion to meet the needs of those to whom the devil dealt a terrible blow. How grateful we were that we connected to the orphanage and those kids at the right time. A few years later, when we visited again, we learned the little girl had died a year after our visit. The other children were thriving, and God continued to heal and restore them. We saw the love and compassion of Jesus at work in the lives of the children and the workers.

Love and compassion are gifts God happily pours into the lives of believers so He can use us to impact lives. The widow did not ask Jesus to perform the miracle. He did it because He loved her. Jesus was not distant but very present in her situation. Love saw her in a broken, sad, lonely, confused, and hopeless state and moved in to rescue her. Christ's love is tender, passionate, and devoted to those who will receive it. When we are compassionate, we are filled with sympathy, tenderness, kindness, mercy, and pity for those struggling. Love and compassion have moved God for centuries to act on behalf of mankind. Even when we sin and fall short of God's standards, love and compassion still extend to us. Some people will not reach out for it but turn away from God in moments of weakness.

God wants you to run to Him and not away from Him, even when you have done wrong. He is a source of peace and strength in your moments of crisis. Love and compassion caused Jesus to set His face like flint as He walked toward the cross. Love and compassion moved Him to send us the Holy Spirit to comfort and help us in our struggles. Love and compassion motivate the God-head and should inspire everything we do. If we desire to perform miracles and the motivation is not love and compassion for hurting humanity, we will miss what God wants to do in and through us.

Love That Heals

Jesus often spoke of God's divine love for mankind. This love is pure, intense, unselfish, and merciful. Matthew 27:37, He taught us to love God with all our hearts, the core of who we are. To love Him with all our soul involves our actions and our attitudes. To love God with all our strength includes our physical and emotional strength, and to love Him with our mind includes our intellect, which is our ability to reason, think, plan, and execute. God never asks us to do anything we are incapable of doing. When He tells us to do something, He has equipped us to do it. So His commandments to us are not grievous. When we love God with the intensity described in Matthew 27, we will begin to love people the way God loves them.

Why is loving others so important to God? Because it is by our love people will come to know Him. When love is our motivation, we will never miss an opportunity to be the hands and feet of Jesus. In 1 John 4:18, Jesus says perfect love casts out fear. The Father's perfect love for us keeps fear from taking up permanent residence in our hearts; the Son's perfect love will stifle the grip of fear that tries to overtake us; the Holy Spirit's perfect love will cast fear out of our hearts and minds and bring comfort to our souls.

When we understand this deep love, fear will never keep us from stepping out in faith and performing the miracles Jesus said we would do. With this great love at work in our hearts, we will be an unstoppable people, running the race with excellence, always focusing on Jesus, the author, and finisher of our faith. Love is the greatest gift God has given us because His Son embodied love. Love is the greatest gift we can give to any broken and wounded person. Love and compassion can profoundly impact a person's life; they can change the course of their destiny.

When Jesus raised the widow's son, He gave them an amazing testimony. Can you imagine the son's testimony? He was dead for who knows how long, and while on the way to the burial, the Son of God called him back to life with tender words of love and compassion. When this young man sat up in the coffin, he came face-to-face with the Son of the all-powerful God. What a life-changing and profound testimony God gave him. This widow did not know she would encounter the lover of her soul on that lonely, sad, devastating walk to the burial site. She had begun the journey because she had no option; her son was dead and needed to be buried. She was greatly suffering even though there were many supporters around her.

How great the love of the Father He would send Jesus into eternity at this precise moment in history to meet her at the point of her greatest need. God's timing was perfect, and Jesus' obedience to the Father connected Him at the right time with God's beloved daughter.

As I think about this amazing story, let me ask a question. What dead thing in your life needs to be raised by Jesus? God will send His Son at the right time to resurrect you just as He did this widow's son. Hold steady—Jesus is on His way to meet you.

Lessons To Live By

- Love and compassion are the ingredients that produce miracles.
- Jesus' miracles in your life will always lift you and elevate you to another level.
- Jesus always encourages the brokenhearted.
- Jesus' name is so powerful that only His spoken words are necessary to create miracles.
- Jesus never leaves us in the broken conditions in which He finds us.
- God has always been involved with the struggles of His children.

A Scripture for Healing – Malachi 4:2

Father, thank You that Your Word says the Sun of Righteousness will arise over those who fear Your name with healing in His wings. Lord, I pray today that Your healing power will flood my life, in Jesus' name.
Amen!

Delivered and Set Free

Our understanding of who Jesus is and what He accomplished by His death on the cross should cause us to give Him unceasing praise and worship.

When we recognize the price, He paid to redeem us, our heartfelt response should be thanksgiving and gratitude. At times we lack the desire to give worship and adoration to the King because we do not fully comprehend how truly worthy He is.

Take a moment and go back to a time when you struggled with sickness, whether in your own body or the body of a loved one. If you cannot recall an illness, how about a financial struggle you faced where you could not put food on the table? Still, for others, it might have been a difficult season in your marriage. Whatever your struggles, you may have felt hopeless at the time. Some struggles appeared impossible, and you could not see a way out. As you faced these situations, a desire to worship God was probably not high on your list of priorities. The reason is that even though sometimes we do not want to admit it, we may blame God for the troubles. We reason since He is all-powerful, He is then able to safeguard our lives and keep us from harm. We often forget we live in a world that is overrun with evil. Because of Adam and Eve's choices, our ancestors' bad decisions, and our choices, the enemy has gained a foothold in our lives and has taken us down a destructive path.

God is not a troublemaker; He does not bring trouble into your life. He is a loving, compassionate Father who is in tune with the well-being of His children. As powerful as God is, our choices prohibit Him from interfering with the many things impacting our lives. When each of us chooses a path that brings about difficulties, He is aware and available to help us get through and overcome them. During our struggles, we often will not worship Him. We can be resentful, bitter, and unforgiving and generally find someone else to blame for our hardship, and it is usually God who gets the blame for what we deem as His inability to help us. We fail to realize that worship is where we find peace and solace from the constant worries of life. Praise will raise you as you praise God over your circumstances.

Our emotional struggles keep us from worshipping the One who can deliver us. I shared in chapter one about my struggle with an ulcer that took years to heal. Not only did I struggle with the physical pain, but also with the emotional pain. My mind was in constant turmoil, even while praying and believing God would heal me. I reasoned it was unthinkable for someone so young (it began at age 16) should be suffering the degree of pain that seemed to plague me constantly. I felt God should not have allowed this to happen to me, and I failed to trust Him in moments of intense pain.

Often in our pain, we do not realize others are also struggling with life issues. Countless people are suffering in hospitals worldwide, including children, and many do not have access to essential medicines to ease their pain. I had medication, and sometimes it eased the pain, but when it did not, I complained. While complaining, I was still praying and asking God to heal me. I was double-minded and unsure about whether God was going to heal me. James 1:8 says a double-minded man is unstable in all His ways. I needed to be steadfast in my faith. I should have nailed down my hope in God, but I had conflict in my heart, and my trust in God eroded. Enduring any type of pain (physical or emotional) is difficult. If we can remain at peace in our seasons of pain, we will have easier days because peace stabilizes us. The peace God gives has the power to sustain us when we are hurting and cannot find the answer.

I have known people who have maintained their hope and joy in the Lord amidst cancer and Lou Garret's disease. They kept on laughing and enjoying life, and their happiness lifted their spirits and those of their caretakers. They truly leaned on God and trusted in His faithful promises. I am reminded of one of my favorite scriptures, which is found in Isaiah 55:10-11: *For as the rain cometh down, and the snow from heaven, and returneth not thither, but watereth the earth, and maketh it bring forth and bud, that it may give seed to the sower, and bread to the eater: So shall my word be that goeth forth out of my mouth: it shall not return unto me void, but it shall accomplish that which I please, and it shall prosper in the thing whereto I sent it.*

Let's look at some of the promises in this scripture:

1. Rain and snow will always fall from heaven.
2. The earth will be watered.
3. The trees will always bring forth fruit.
4. Those who sow will eat and enjoy what they have sown.
5. God's Word and promises will not return to us empty.
6. Each promise will produce results in our lives.
7. God's Word will accomplish what pleases Him.

8. God's Word will prosper wherever He has sent it.

These assurances in His Word and promises are as sure as rain, snow, the earth being watered, and trees producing fruit. These things have happened for centuries and will continue to happen even when we are no longer here. God's Word will stand throughout the ages. His Word never gets old, and it is life-sustaining. As you speak God's Word over your situation, it must produce results in your life. His Word cannot return to you empty because it is pregnant with the life of God. Everything God does is filled with life-giving blessings for His children. When you pray, it is impossible not to receive your heart's sincere petitions. God will hear and answer our cries for help. Even though some of the answers may not be immediate, He will respond if we wait in faith and with expectancy. In the waiting, we can be assured He will do what He has promised.

There is no benefit in getting upset or having a bad attitude toward God because you will not get the desired results. Having a bad attitude will add to the delay, as God will need to do further work in your heart to get you to become the person He wants you to be. Take it from someone who has been there. It is best to wait, hope, pray, and trust God for His promises to manifest in your life. A thankful heart, even when you do not understand the process, will move God to act in your situation.

When it is hardest to worship in these seasons, do it anyway. If all you can do is raise one hand, lift it and tell God, "Lord, I don't feel like worshipping during this trial, but You are worth it." We do not worship God just because things are wonderful in our life and world; we worship Him despite it all because He is indeed worthy. Often when you decide to worship, you will not feel like it. Worship is never about a feeling; it is about a God deserving it. Worship has nothing to do with our emotions but has everything to do with how we demonstrate our trust in God, no matter what we are facing. Lifting one hand is an act of surrendering to His Lordship. You will discover that lifting the second hand and bowing your knees will become much easier because you recognize He is a faithful Father.

Transforming Worship

In Mark chapter 5, Jesus met a man completely possessed by evil spirits. Yet, even in his demented state, the man came and fell at the feet of Jesus in worship.

Then they came to the other side of the sea, to the region of the Gerasenes. As soon as He got out of the boat, a man with an unclean spirit came out of the tombs and met Him. He lived in the tombs. No one was able to restrain him anymore - even with chains - because he had often been bound with shackles and chains, but had snapped off the chains and smashed the shackles. No one was strong enough to subdue him. And always, night and day, he was crying out among the tombs and in the mountains and cutting himself with stones. When he saw Jesus from a distance, he ran and knelt before Him. And he cried out with a loud voice, "What do you have to do with me, Jesus, Son of the Most High God? I beg you before God, don't torment me!" For He had told him, "Come out of the man, you unclean spirit!" "What is your name?" He asked him. "My name is Legion," he answered Him, "because we are many." And he kept begging Him not to send them out of the region. Now a large herd of pigs was there, feeding on the hillside. The demons begged Him, "Send us to the pigs, so we may enter them." And He gave them permission. Then the unclean spirits came out and entered the pigs, and the herd of about 2,000 rushed down the steep bank into the sea and drowned there.

Mark 5:1-13 (HCSB)

This scripture shows us Jesus will be worshipped even by those who do not claim Him as Lord. We can glean from this story that there is power in the name of Jesus, and evil spirits will acknowledge it and are also subject to Him. I am convinced every place Jesus went while He was on earth was an ordained place. He was ordained to be there at the right time to make a difference in the lives of the people He met. The meeting with this demon-possessed man was ordained. God had explicitly assigned Jesus to intersect with this man in a desperate situation. In setting man free, God demonstrated that all power is His alone and everything in heaven and earth is subject to Him.

As we look at this story, we again see the love and compassion of the Father for the lost. The Gerasenes were near the east coast by the Sea of Galilee. Most of the people in the region were Gentile farmers who raised pigs. Pigs were considered unclean by the Jews, who would have nothing to do with them. When Jesus stepped out of the boat, one of the first people to greet Him was a man who lived among the tombs. He lived there because he was possessed by the devil and could not live in a normal environment with other people. The tombs where he lived were caves.

We can hardly begin to imagine the condition of this man's life. The enemy had total control of his mind. He did not act normally and hence, lived in the caves. He most likely scared those who encountered him, so as a result, he lived in a place where very few people would venture. This man lived in darkness because his soul was inhabited by darkness. The light of God was absent in the darkness of his soul and the dark place where he lived. When the light of the Son is not in our lives, we become lost and can be possessed and harmed by the devil. We need Jesus, the Light, to fill our hearts, so the devil has no entry point. Light and darkness cannot exist together. Light will always overtake and dispel darkness.

The Bible does not tell us how the man became so possessed by the devil. What is apparent is a door was opened in his life that allowed the enemy access to him. This door could have been one he opened himself because of sin, or it could have been a generational sin that opened the door in his life. Whatever the cause, he was wholly possessed. No one was able to restrain him. He had tremendous strength and destroyed the shackles and chains they used to bind him.

One thing is clear this man was in a desperate situation. Day and night, he cried out because he was so tormented. He cut himself with stones, probably trying to anesthetize his pain. Consider the Father's love for this man that He would reach down to him in his torment. As God listened to his cries, He sent the Deliver, who was initially sent to the Jewish people and not to the Gentile race. Remember, this region where Jesus went was inhabited by Gentiles. Jesus went out of His way to intersect with this man to bring him deliverance. The Bible tells us Jesus is touched by the feelings of our infirmities (Hebrews 4:15). He is touched because the Father in Heaven is in touch with our infirmities. In his torment, the man recognized his day of deliverance. He recognized Jesus from a great distance and ran from the tombs and the darkness to meet the Light. He was not casual in approaching Jesus; he used all his strength to get to Him. His running speaks of his desperation and need. How did this demon-possessed man recognize Jesus? The evil spirits living in Him knew the Son of God because they lived in heaven and served as angels before they were kicked out with the devil.

The first thing the man did was kneel at the feet of Jesus. He worshipped! In his torment, with all the evil spirits living in him, he could not help but bow his knees to the One True King. The evil spirits who had kept him in torment for all those years could not keep him from bowing down to the Master. Light came into his dark world, and he recognized the True Light. Not only did he recognize the light, but he also responded to it.

Now, consider that for many years this man could not control his actions and was subject to the whims of the evil spirits that possessed him; yet, when Jesus came on the scene, the evil spirits could not restrain him. They were unable to control his reaction to the appearance of the Savior. The evil spirits had to bow before the One with all power and authority in His hands. As the man knelt before Jesus, one of the spirits asked, "What do you have to do with me, Jesus, Son of the Most High God?" He used the complete title for Jesus.

I said earlier the spirits recognized Jesus because they had previously served the Most High God. You may recall when the devil decided to challenge God and attempted to take His Throne, God threw him and one-third of the angels out of heaven. These angels became the evil spirits who now roam the earth and serve the devil. They attempt to oppose God, and wherever they see an opening, they will try to take possession of a person causing them to become insane, dumb, or even blind. Their control can be so deep-seated the person may become suicidal.

The evil spirit who spoke begged Jesus not to torment him. At least 2,000 demons possessed this man because that was the total number of pigs they entered after Jesus evicted them. Although many evil spirits possessed him, one spirit appeared to be the leader, the spokesperson. After acknowledging Jesus, the demon requested Jesus not torment him. How did Jesus torment the evil spirit? The brilliance and power of His presence were too great for it. Every evil thing will be exposed wherever there is light, and these spirits are exposed. They knew they had no option but to leave this man because all authority and power were in the hands of Jesus. They were not yet ready to leave the 'house' where they had lived for years, but they were given no choice. When you meet Jesus, you will be changed regardless of what spirit controls you.

After their eviction, the evil spirits understood they would have to give an account to their leader, the devil. I am convinced they were not looking forward to explaining why they could not remain in the man. It would be an unpleasant task. I can imagine their fear when they faced the devil and told him Jesus, the Son of the Most High God, showed up and commanded them to leave. It was another reminder that there was One who was greater and more powerful than he. The devil's control over the people in the region was broken because Jesus came and set the captive free. Therefore, the people knew there was a Deliverer (Jesus) in the land.

I have not found many instances in the Word where Jesus had conversations with evil spirits. He generally commands them to leave, and they go. However, in this story, He asked this spirit his name. The spirit said his name was Legion because there were many. By asking this question, Jesus gives us insight into what goes on in the spirit world and the lives of those the enemy possesses. When we meet people who need healing, we must find out the source of the problem if we can. Many physical ailments can be a direct result of some demonic activity. When Jesus asked the spirit how many of them were in the man, he knew the answer. He provided an example for us to follow. We cannot assume we are only dealing with one evil spirit in a person's life because others may be present.

Someone once told me when you meet a demon-possessed person and can quickly discern what spirit is at work in the person, be sure to ask God to reveal all activities because there are usually more spirits hiding behind the visible one. This is what Jesus did by asking the name of the evil spirit. He saw the horrific condition of the man and knew there had to be more than one spirit at work in him.

Since the evil spirits had no option but to leave, they begged to be sent into the pigs. Jesus gave permission, knowing the pigs would drown themselves in the end. Think about this for a moment. If the two thousand pigs had only one evil spirit enter each pig, and they all fled down the mountain and drowned themselves, how could one man stay alive with all those evil spirits possessing him? The answer is simple. God! God sustained him even in his tormented state until his Deliver came because this would demonstrate His power to the people. When Jesus came, the man recognized his help had arrived and did not stay away. He ran with all his might toward Him and received his freedom.

Jesus is our Deliverer and Healer. When He delivers and heals, He always shows us that we are free. We will experience freedom from pain in our bodies, and our minds will be free from further torment. In allowing this man to witness the pigs' drowning, Jesus showed him he was free from all demonic possession. If and when the evil spirits try to return and test him by telling him he is not free, he would have a visible reminder of the pigs. He would remember the pigs were so overcome with demonic possession they killed themselves. This demonstration was a marker in his life that Jesus had wholly delivered him and a warning not to become entangled again with whatever caused the problem in the first place.

The Commission

Just before Jesus ascended into heaven, He commissioned all believers. According to Mark 16:17, "And these signs shall follow them that believe; In my name shall they cast out devils; they shall speak with new tongues; They shall take up serpents; and if they drink any deadly thing, it shall not hurt them; they shall lay hands on the sick, and they shall recover." My purpose in sharing this scripture is to highlight the first thing Jesus mentioned in the great commission. He told them, first and foremost, they will drive out devils. I believe the message to us is that if we do not drive out the devils, people will not be able to retain their healing and freedom. God gave similar instructions to the Israelites in Numbers 33:55. The Israelites were to dispossess the inhabitants of the land God gave them as their possession.

We must ensure people's hearts and minds are cleansed first so the devil no longer has a foothold in their lives. Jesus tells us to drive out the devil. He wants us to be free from constant harassment and torment. Jesus does not want our minds and emotions to be controlled by the devil's whim. He knows if we continue to live in concert with the devil, he will ultimately destroy us.

In freeing this man, Jesus demonstrated God's desire to bring freedom and healing to all people. God is not partial in His love for mankind. Although He initially sent Jesus to the Jewish people, He has since included us Gentiles to be partakers of the blessings of being His children. We will ultimately experience freedom when our minds are released from the enemy's grip. We must drive the enemy and evil spirits out of our lives, churches, cities, and nations by using the powerful name of Jesus and the authority He has given us. As you look around, I am sure the enemy has many people in his grip. Even those who profess to be Christians, which translates into 'Christ Ones,' are caught up in the enemy's traps because they have believed his lies. The devil and evil spirits are committing the atrocities we see in our world. The devil is determined to destroy us and nullify our relationship with God. The lies and unwholesome suggestions the enemy whispers in your ears are designed to keep you away from the presence of God. Do not be fooled or led astray by the devil.

As I think about the horrific penalty of sin and the death of

Jesus on the cross, I am reminded that God would not have sent His beloved Son to pay such an exorbitant price if you and I could continue to live sinful lives and still inherit His Kingdom. The sacrifice of Jesus would be wasted if we were allowed access to heaven and eternal life while continuing in habitual sin. The devil has perpetuated the lie that we can live ungodly, immoral lives and still enter the Kingdom of God, and many believers are buying into it.

Remember, in Luke 11:15-20, Jesus is falsely accused of being possessed by the devil. What was His response? "Every kingdom divided against itself is brought to desolation, and a house divided against a house falleth. If Satan also is divided against himself, how shall his kingdom stand? Because ye say that I cast out devils through Beelzebub. And if I by Beelzebub cast out devils, by whom do your sons cast them out? Therefore shall they be your judges? But if I by the finger of God cast out devils, no doubt the kingdom of God is come upon you." This scripture makes a clear distinction between God and Satan. If we try to serve God and the devil, we will not succeed because our loyalty will be divided, and division will cause destruction. When we truly serve God—when He has all of our heart, soul, and mind—we will only desire to do what He commands us to do. If our loyalty is divided, we will not be able to stand against the evil around us. If we are not totally and completely sold out to God, we will not make a stand for Him. You cannot win if God is against you. God asks, "If He is for you, who can be against you?" No one! God was for the demon-possessed man, and not even the devil and thousands of evil spirits could ultimately destroy him. God is for you. He is with you in your struggles. God hears every cry and groan and weeps with you. He listened to the demon-possessed man's cries and sent Him a Deliver and Healer. He will always respond to you and send you help.

Lessons To Live By

- God always hears your cries for help.
- He is with you in the crises of life.
- The feelings of your infirmities touch Him.
- He wants to free you.
- He will allow others to witness your victory.
- He is your Deliver.
- He is an ever-present help in times of trouble.
- Worship Him even when you don't feel like it because it will lift the burdens off your shoulders.

A Scripture for Healing – 3 John 1:2

Father, in the name of Jesus, I thank You for Your promise in 3 John 1:2, which says, "Beloved, I wish above all things that thou mayest prosper and be in health, even as thy soul prospers." Father, thank You that it is Your desire that I prosper in every area of my life. You desire that I prosper (be in health) in my mind, soul, emotions, body, and spirit. I receive Your prosperity in my entire life today,
in Jesus' name.
Amen!

Healing a Beloved Servant

Have you ever had a close friend who desires the best for you? They have supported you and will go to any lengths to see you prosper and succeed. They have been your cheerleader, advocate, and encourager through all your struggles.

When you felt like giving up, they were there to remind you that your outcome would be great because Jesus already gave you the victory. When you have someone like that in your corner, it is impossible not to succeed.

In Luke 7, we find a story of a Roman officer who went out of his way to secure help for a beloved servant. The servant was not a close friend or a family member; he was just someone who served this officer. I would venture to say the servant must have been outstanding because he was respected by those he served. The Roman officer cared deeply about the servant's well-being and desired him to be healed. This Roman officer oversaw more than one hundred soldiers, yet, he took time out of his busy schedule to see about this servant who meant so much to him. This example speaks of the servant's devotion to those he served and how he won their hearts and respect through this devotion.

God will give us opportunities to shine in everything He assigns us to do. Whatever situation or circumstance you find yourself in, there will always be times when you will be tested and tried to see what comes out of your heart.

I do not believe many of us, including this servant, would willingly spend our days serving others in what some in our society would consider the lowest of vocations if we had other options. Yet, in this lowly position, the servant shone. His service was outstanding, so his leader did all he could to ensure he got well when he became sick. Let's examine this scripture to see what was in the heart of the Roman officer toward this servant.

Now when he had ended all his sayings in the audience of the people, he entered into Capernaum. And a certain centurion's servant, who was dear unto him, was sick, and ready to die. And when he heard of Jesus, he sent unto him the elders of the Jews, beseeching him that he would come and heal his servant. And when they came to Jesus, they besought him instantly, saying, That he was worthy for whom he should do this: For he loveth our nation, and he hath built us a synagogue. Then Jesus went with them. And when he was now not far from the house, the centurion sent friends to him, saying unto him, Lord, trouble not thyself: for I am not worthy that thou shouldest enter under my roof: Wherefore neither thought I myself worthy to come unto thee: but say in a word, and my servant shall be healed. For I also am a man set under authority, having under me soldiers, and I say unto one, Go, and he goeth; and to another, Come, and he cometh; and to my servant, Do this, and he doeth it. When Jesus heard these things, he marveled at him, and turned him about, and said unto the people that followed him, I say unto you, I have not found so great faith, no, not in Israel.
Luke 7:1-9 (KJV)

Jesus had finished ministering and sharing some great parables with His followers, and after His teaching, He decided to journey to Capernaum. When He arrived in Capernaum, He encountered this soldier and the people who wanted this servant healed. In this story in Luke 7, we see a servant beloved by his master and those around him. We also find a centurion who seemed to have a good relationship with the Jewish elders and sent them to Jesus because he was concerned for his servant's health. These Jews spoke highly of the centurion, which was unusual because these Roman soldiers were generally brutal to the people and showed a lack of mercy toward men, women, and children. The Jewish elders told Jesus the Roman officer was worthy to make this request of Him. The officer had impacted the lives of the Jewish people in a significant way. He had built them a synagogue for worship even though he had no personal relationship with their God. This story is a reminder that God is always working in the hearts of men and women.

Those who seem to be the most difficult to reach with the love of Jesus can be reached when God begins to break up the hard places in their hearts. When we think about our loved ones with whom we desire to come into a relationship with Jesus Christ, we may feel hopeless at times, but God is faithful to bring this to pass. God can reach those who appear not to know Him. Proverb 21:1 says that the king's heart is in God's hand, turning it as He wills. God can and will change the hearts of your family members. He promised in Acts 16:31 that our household would be saved. Since He has promised this, you can be assured He will bring their salvation to pass. All His promises to us are yes and amen.

In the story of the Roman officer's devotion, it is evident he saw something of great value in the servant and the Jewish elders. What he saw in them softened his heart toward them. The synagogue he built for the Jews was one of the places where Jesus often taught the Word when He was in Capernaum. In Mark 1:21-25,

Jesus healed a demon-possessed man in this synagogue. I am convinced the soldier heard the report of Jesus and His work among the Jews. This soldier befriended the Jews, which was different from what the other soldiers had done. Through his relationship with them, he heard about Jesus and the miracles He performed in the lives of so many people; hence, the reason he sent for Him.

The officer valued his servant as a beloved son, not a servant, so he went out of his way to help him. The officer did not have the attitude that if the servant died, he could find a better replacement. The servant was not easily replaceable in the eyes of his master. He wanted his servant well, not just to continue his service, but because he was a valuable and beloved person.

Considering the above statement, what value do you place on your family or loved ones? What is the value of those who serve you, whether in your home or on the job? Do you see them for who they truly are, precious in the eyes of God, or are they easily replaceable to you? I have found that many of us do not place a high value on the people God has placed in our lives.

Several years ago, the Lord gave me a message to teach at a Bible Study on the value of our family members. Before preparing the message, He had me observe how people act at church, both with their brothers and sisters in Christ and with strangers. They are generally friendly, loving, and encouraging, and sometimes can go overboard trying to be helpful. In counseling some of these people's relatives, spouses, and children, you find the story is entirely different at home when dealing with their loved ones. Often some of these individuals who appear to be helpful to others can be impatient, harsh, critical, and unfriendly to their loved ones.

God gave me the assignment of challenging each person to consider that their spouses and children are gifts from God who are only on loan to them for a short time while on earth. Then, He shared that there are no marriages in heaven for believers, and we will be like the angels (Matthew 22:30). With that picture in mind, He reminded us we are all brothers and sisters in Christ. God challenged us to look at how we treat our brothers and sisters who live in our homes and serve on our jobs. He questioned why we would honor those in the church more than those in our homes. He reminded us we are all one in Christ Jesus, and when we get to heaven, those of our family members whom we treated unjustly will only have the role of being our brothers and sisters in Christ. That is the ultimate relationship for all Christians, and it should cause us to remember to honor those He honors and love and respect those He has placed in our lives. Jesus is our elder brother, and we are joint heirs with Him.

The servant was not part of the centurion's family, but he honored him anyway. The Centurion's care for his servant speaks of devotion to someone considered the most minor in his household. This is the level of respect God wants us to give to people.

The Request

Remember, the Roman officer sent the Jewish elders to ask Jesus to come and heal his servant. After Jesus heard the request and praise for the officer and the servant, He began His journey to the home. While Jesus was a short distance away, the centurion sent some of his friends to tell Jesus he was not worthy for Him to come to his home. You can see and feel the turmoil that must have taken place in the mind and heart of this officer. He felt unworthy of having Jesus come to his home. He probably thought of all the wrongs he had committed and concluded since Jesus was all-powerful, He was well aware of his sins. Like us, the enemy harassed this officer's mind by reminding him of his past actions, sins, and offenses. The more the officer reflected on his shortcomings, the more unworthy he felt, which led him to tell Jesus not to come even though He was only a short distance away.

I am reminded of the prophet Isaiah whom we are told in Isaiah 6:1-8 also discovered some things about himself after his earthly king died. Isaiah saw the Lord clearly for the first time, and when he came face-to-face with Him, he remembered how sinful he and the people around him were, and he felt unworthy to be in the presence of the King.

When we truly recognize who Jesus is, we are reminded of who we are and how unworthy we were before Him saving and changing us. Like Isaiah and the Roman officer, we must examine our hearts to ensure that King Jesus is welcome at any time. It should be our greatest desire that Jesus is welcomed into our lives so that He may have the freedom to reign fully in us.

At first, the officer sent the Jewish elders to bring Jesus to his home, but when he changed his mind after feeling unworthy, he did not send the elders; he called and sent his friends. Let's examine this. Why did he send his friends instead of other elders to Jesus? He would have to give them a reason for his change of heart. It would be difficult for this officer to share with strangers that although he was the leader of many, he did not feel worthy to meet Jesus face-to-face. That would expose his insecurities, and he was unwilling to make himself vulnerable before strangers.

When we feel insecure, sharing these feelings with family and friends is easier than with strangers. True friends will not judge but will encourage you when you feel most vulnerable. This officer was no different from us. He went to those who would cover him in his weaknesses and those who would understand his discomfort. We seldom share our struggles with people we are not in close relationships with because we are unsure if they will have our backs and provide coverage when we need it. Those who genuinely love us will usually listen and not be judgmental or critical amid our uncertainty. His friends understood him and made the journey to meet with Jesus.

The Response

I said earlier Jesus, upon hearing the request, began the journey to the centurion's home. He had listened to the concerns of the Jewish elders and was moved to go and heal the servant. I love Jesus because He is no respecter of persons. No matter who expresses their need for Him, He is always available to them. He was quick to respond upon hearing this servant needed healing. The servant's name was not given, but his station in life was clear. This did not deter Jesus. He had equal respect for all people and treated those who had influence and position the same way He treated those who had none. He loves and serves all people equally.

When the centurion's friends reached Jesus, they told Him of the officer's change of heart and shared their friend's words. The officer said to tell Jesus, "But speak the word, and my servant will be healed. For I myself am a man under authority, with soldiers under me. I tell this one to go, and he goes, and that one come and he comes. I say to my servant do this and he does it."

Upon hearing these words, Jesus was amazed and shared His amazement with the crowd. Jesus heard something extraordinary in the officer's words. He had finally encountered someone who understood authority. This officer understood being under the authority of his leaders first and then having authority over those he led.

Jesus marveled that He had not found such great faith in the Jewish people or their leaders. Nowhere in Jerusalem had He met anyone before this officer who understood the power of operating in authority. This officer completely understood when you have authority over anything; it is subject to you.

Along with whatever you have been put in charge of— whether it is leading a team of people, overseeing a project, managing a company, parenting, or teaching— comes delegated authority, so you can make decisions and enforce the rules by which people will live. Those who do not understand authority will never fully accomplish all that has been assigned. People are often timid about moving in any direction because of fear of not making the right decision. At other times, we give people titles but do not give them the authority to make the appropriate decisions when necessary. As a result, this can make a leader timid and hesitant about moving forward or even fearful of making mistakes when required to lead. In these instances, leaders can look uncertain and insecure to those whom they lead, which can cause a lack of respect for that leader.

When you have been given authority and know you have the proper backing, you will not be hesitant to try new things or move in a new direction. People like this officer who understood who he was, his role, and who was assigned to serve him will always be successful because they can make decisions and grow and flourish in the assignment.

Over the years, I have served in several organizations and various management positions and witnessed the misuse of authority. I have seen many instances where people are given authority to lead others and do not even have basic people skills. As a result, their leadership is crippling to those who serve with them. I am always amazed when I find people in management positions who do not know the first thing about standing up for their team. They do not understand taking the heat when something goes wrong with an assignment given to one of their team members. Instead of understanding the team's successes and failures, I have seen many occasions where leaders point the blame exclusively to the person who may have done the work incorrectly. They did not realize that in the final analysis, they, as a leader, were responsible for the outcome of any project assigned to those whom they led.

This officer understood his responsibility to his servant. His authority was entrusted to him, and as a result, he understood the authority delegated to Jesus by God, the Father. Jesus had the authority to speak to anything on earth, and it would obey Him. Jesus marveled at this man's insight, faith level, and confidence in the spoken Word. He discovered a depth of faith in a man who did not know God the Father, who has all authority in His hands.

The officer instinctively knew that all Jesus had to do was speak the words, and his servant would be healed. Jesus did not need to see the servant, touch him, or pray over him for the miracle to occur. The authority in His words was backed by heaven, and everything under the sound of Jesus' voice had to respond to that authority and align itself with His spoken words. Therefore, Jesus did not continue to the house but just spoke the Word, transcending time and space and bringing life to the servant's body. Because this officer understood authority, the things he had heard about Jesus caused him to recognize the One who had actual authority in His hands. The centurion's faith brought healing to his servant and provides a testimony that our faith can produce results every time.

The Believer's Authority

There is a high level of authority that every believer can and should operate in. At this level of authority, we can be just like Jesus in the sense that when we speak, heaven will back us and everything on the earth will line up with our requests. The

Roman officer received the victory and experienced firsthand the power of Jesus because he understood his authority. The Bible does not say, but I am convinced that the Roman officer came to know Jesus as Messiah.

As God's Son, Jesus has been given all authority, and He has turned this authority over to us, the believers. Jesus understood He was under the authority of the Father and operated entirely in it to accomplish God's plans on earth. Jesus only said what He heard His Father say and only did what He saw His Father do. The Spirit of God led him.

Jesus is our example. We are to be led by the Spirit of God and the Word of God as Jesus was while He was on earth. As His followers, we must understand what Jesus has given us and begin to operate in it. The centurion, a non-Jewish person—a non-believer—understood Jesus had the authority and power to heal the sick, cleanse the leper, raise the dead, and set the captives free, and he acted on that belief. Many believers are still struggling to understand and embrace this. As a result of this lack of belief, our lives are powerless, and we are often ineffective at thwarting the enemy's plans and tactics.

As we look at the centurion's wisdom, we see he understood and recognized that Jesus' authority had no boundaries. Therefore, the believers' authority is limitless as well. We can tap into the power of Jesus and begin seeing changes in our lives and those around us.

The challenge for all believers is to speak the Word and then watch the healings manifest. We must speak the Word over sickness, lack, debt, and any other situation that has us in bondage. As we speak the Word, resurrection life will be poured into our problems, and freedom will come to us. In John 11, Jesus spoke the word, and Lazarus rose from the dead. The words He spoke reached beyond the confines of death, into the supernatural realm, and called Lazarus' spirit back to his body. The spoken word, backed with the authority of Jesus, will always produce the right results in your life.

It must have been a joyous occasion for Jesus to finally meet a person on His journey who had unwavering faith and complete knowledge of how to use his authority effectively. The moment was perfect for Jesus to deliver the message He had been trying to convey – that all authority and power were in His hands. Remember, He has given us authority to heal the sick, raise the dead, cleanse the leper, and set the captives free. We have the authority to use the name of Jesus, apply His blood over difficult situations, boldly come before God, and make our petitions known to Him.

Did you notice God did not tell us the name or type of sickness that attacked the servant? I believe it was not given a name to show us even a nameless disease must bow to the name and authority of the Lord Jesus Christ. The challenging circumstances in your life must also bow down each time the name of Jesus is invoked. As we begin to operate in our authority, all of heaven and hell will recognize that we are anointed and appointed by God to be more than conquerors in life.

Our faith, coupled with the authority given by Jesus, will bring healing and wholeness to our lives and deliverance to many who need to encounter the Savior.

Lessons To Live By

- Having a sincere love for others will bring miracles to their lives.
- God is no respecter of persons. He will heal where He finds faith.
- Faith is a requirement for those who want to see miracles.
- We must understand our authority in Christ and begin to operate in it.
- We must willingly step out of our comfort zone to meet the needs of others.
- Though we feel unworthy, Jesus has made us worthy through His sacrifice.
- Having a heart of humility is the ingredient for producing miracles.

A Scripture for Healing – Jeremiah 33:6

Father, I thank You that Your Word says that You will bring health and healing to our lives. You also promise that You will not only heal us but will reveal to us Your abundance of peace. We ask You to please heal us today and fill us with Your amazing peace, in Jesus' name.
Amen!

Healing that Leads to Worship

Have you ever wondered about all the blessings Jesus died to give us? He not only came to give us eternal life but also to heal our broken hearts. His salvation was not in part but whole. Let me explain this statement.

The Greek word for salvation is "Sozo." Sozo means to save, heal, deliver, preserve, protect, make well, and make whole. Wow! Jesus was purposeful in His desire to set us free not only from physical pain but from emotional bondages as well.

When He set His face like flint on the way to the cross (Luke 9:51), He knew we would have many difficulties to overcome in our lives. When you are suffering, physically or emotionally, it is tough to focus on what you are called to do. Jesus provides healing because as we walk in freedom from the things that keep us in bondage, we can serve Him in the fullness of joy. He wants to deliver us from the many traps and pitfalls the enemy has set up along life's journey. These things can be stumbling blocks along the way. He is intent on preserving our sanity and protecting our hearts and emotions from being ravished by the evil one. He protects our hearts and feelings through the provisions He has given in His Word. The Bible says if we call upon the name of the Lord, we shall be saved (Romans 10:13). Again, He will Sozo us—heal, deliver, preserve, and protect us. The Word is the antidote for every trial we face. I have discovered a scripture, an answer, in the Bible for every difficulty you and I will ever endure.

Not only did Jesus come to save and set us free from sin and eternal damnation, but He bore our sicknesses and diseases on the cross. I have read there are thirty-nine root causes for diseases on the earth. Therefore, for every stripe Jesus took on His back, He bore one that you may be healed. As you pursue God for your healing, remember every sickness and disease was nailed to the cross. Whenever I come under attack in my body or even in my emotions, I quickly remind God of the stripes Jesus bore so I do not have to endure this suffering. I remember the crown of thorns that pierced His brow, and I recall His intense suffering gives me access to healing for my mind and emotions. What an amazing Savior and a wonderful gift of healing to our wounded souls! He wants us to be well, and He wants to make us whole. He desires that nothing remains broken in our bodies and our minds. Jesus came to mend broken hearts and broken lives.

Have you ever ministered to someone who still gives glory to God while in excruciating pain? I have left that experience examining myself to see if I readily praise God while in pain or if I spend more time complaining instead of praising. A few years ago, I went to Jamaica to visit my family. During the trip, I saw my uncle, who was very sick and in constant pain, and he was hooked up to machines to ease some of his suffering. Since I was a child, this uncle had been a Pastor who loved to minister the Word of God. I intended to encourage him in his struggles, but I was the one who received encouragement. From the moment I stepped into the house, he began to share the Word and his deep and abiding love for Jesus Christ

In the hours I spent with him, he testified about how God

saved him; the hundreds of people who had come to faith in Jesus because God used him in his small community; and about the hundreds more whom he had the privilege of baptizing in the name of the Lord Jesus Christ. Midway through our conversation, he turned and asked me, "Young lady, are you saved, and do you know Jesus?" He was not shy about asking me this question but was bold and direct in his approach. When I responded I was indeed saved, he began to dig deeper to see if I was indeed sold out to Christ and fully living for Him. He gave praise, worship, and thanksgiving to God for saving him and using his life in such a profound way. With very little education, he had learned the Bible and taught it to many. As he sat in the tiny home that was falling apart around him (he was alone most days and nights because his wife had been dead for many years), he talked of his longing to meet his Savior and to fellowship with Jesus face-to-face. I was touched that amid such great suffering, all this man did was give glory to God. Even as I write this segment, I cannot contain the tears; his story so impacts me. I am challenged to know and love the Savior with the same depth and devotion as this great man. He died a year after our visit, and I know his welcome by the Savior was spectacular.

I look forward to meeting him again in heaven one day because he is definitely in my future, not my past. After all, he was saved. In his pain and suffering, he took time to worship God.

A Cry for Help

Let us look at an example in Luke 17 of what happens when we worship God during crises.

And it came to pass, as he went to Jerusalem, that he passed through

the midst of Samaria and Galilee. And as he entered into a certain
village, there met him ten men that were lepers, which stood afar off:
And they lifted up their voices, and said, Jesus, Master, have mercy
on us. And when he saw them, he said unto them, Go show yourselves
unto the priests. And it came to pass, that, as they went, they were
cleansed. And one of them, when he saw that he was healed, turned
back, and with a loud voice glorified God, And fell down on his face
at his feet, giving him thanks: and he was a Samaritan. And Jesus
answering said, Were there not ten cleansed? but where are the
nine? There are not found that returned to give glory to God, save
this stranger. And he said unto him, Arise, go thy way: thy faith
hath made thee whole.
Luke 17:11-19 (NVJ)

This story is a prime example of how often we neglect to thank God for all the wonderful things He has done in our lives. We often pray, petition, beg, and plead for His help; however, when He moves in our circumstances, we say a quick thank you and then carry on with our busy lives and forget His powerful move. When God does something extraordinary in your life, you should never forget it. This is a marker, a memorial of His promises being fulfilled in your life. I believe we should go back often and reflect on how God has delivered us, provided for us, and how He has been our ever-present help in times of trouble.

The story of these ten lepers teaches valuable lessons to those who want to receive all God desires to deposit in their lives. Ask the Lord to examine your heart and motives as you read it. Jesus was on His way to Jerusalem when He met the lepers. He had just finished ministering to the disciples about having faith the size of a grain of mustard seed. He had talked with them about a master-servant relationship. He said a servant, no matter how hard he has worked, is still expected to serve his master even when he is tired and before he has eaten. Jesus was sharing with the disciples, and with us specific duties we must perform. These duties are not optional in our lives; they are mandatory and must be completed. He took it a step further. He said once the servant has served the master, the master does not thank him because the servant is simply doing his job. The servant's responsibility is to provide reasonable service to his master.

Our reasonable service to the Master is to give thanks no matter the circumstance. His lesson to the disciples and us is when we have completed the things we are commanded to do; we are only doing what was assigned to us. Often we forget we are required to do significant things with the lives Jesus paid such an exorbitant price to redeem. The Bible says we are bought with a price and must glorify God with our bodies (1 Corinthian 6:20).

Jesus shared these profound lessons on service with the disciples just before He encountered the lepers. When He healed them, and only one returned to say thanks, how impactful the message must have been since it was still fresh in their minds. In this teaching, He taught them about responsibility toward others, the need for forgiveness, operating in faith, and the dangers of being caught up in obligations. Let's examine the impact of leprosy on a person's life.

As previously shared, leprosy is a skin disease that is contagious and incurable. It attacks the whole body. When Jesus met these lepers, they were outcasts in their society. They were not allowed to live in the same home with their families, nor were they allowed to mix with others. As a result, they lived in a leper colony. Leprosy caused isolation for those who were suffering. When a leper is removed from society, they lose everything—family, job, home, possessions, and dignity—a person with leprosy experiences much shame and embarrassment. To be identified as lepers, these people had to wear torn clothes, their hair had to be unkept, and they were required to cover the lower part of their faces. If that was not enough, they had to cry loudly, "Unclean, unclean," so people would not get near them and possibly catch the disease. How painful and humiliating to have once been a part of society, and now you are an outcast.

The lepers' families could not talk face-to-face or touch them. Since the disease was considered unclean, a Jewish person could not touch a leper, or they would be defiled just as if they had touched a dead person. It was believed leprosy was a sign of God's disfavor upon a person's life.

Do you recall in Numbers chapter 12, Aaron and Miriam began to speak against Moses because he had married a Cushite woman? They disapproved of his choice for a wife because the Cushites were descendants of Kush, aka Nubia, from the northeast of Africa. The nations of Africa were identified with Ham, the son of Noah, and they are dark-skinned people. Miriam and Aaron were dealing with prejudice against Moses' wife. They began to question if the Lord had only spoken through Moses and said God had also spoken to them. It is apparent they were setting the stage to overthrow Moses. They wanted his leadership position; they wanted to be the ones to lead the people of God.

God was very displeased when He heard this because He had appointed Moses, so He intervened dramatically. God told Moses, Aaron, and Miriam to come to the Tent of Meeting, and He descended in a pillar of clouds. God came personally to deal with their rebellion and lack of submission to the authority He had established over them. In their conversation, God says something profound about Moses. He told them He generally speaks to prophets in dreams and visions, but to Moses, He speaks face-to-face because Moses was faithful in all His house. God then challenged Aaron and Miriam about why they were not afraid to speak against His servant Moses.

The Bible says the anger of the Lord burned against them, and when He left their presence and the cloud lifted, Miriam was covered with leprosy and was as white as snow. God showed His disfavor with her. Why Miriam and not also Aaron? I believe she was probably the ringleader and the one who pushed Aaron into this rebellion. Aaron was also quick to repent. Moses cried out to God for her healing; God's response was priceless. He said, "If her father had spit in her face, would she not have been in disgrace for seven days? Confine her outside the camp for seven days; after that, she can be brought back." All the Israelites witnessed her shame, disgrace, and punishment. She was an outcast and could not communicate and fellowship with the people because she was contagious. The people saw the tremendous cost of speaking against the man of God, and it was a clear warning to them not to speak against God's chosen leader.

Now let's get back to the story of the ten lepers. In Jesus' century, when people with leprosy went to the synagogue to worship, they had to sit in a specially assigned place six feet from other people. They had to arrive first and were the last ones to leave. They were in a challenging and trying situation. While dealing with all these struggles, they were also dealing with people who believed their leprosy was a sign of God's disfavor, so we can be sure that people constantly whispered and talked about them. The lepers stayed in groups to provide support for one another. When they cried out to Jesus, they did it from a distance. They did not approach Him because they knew their boundaries. Their cries reached His ears, and He responded to them with love and compassion.

A Merciful Savior

When the lepers cried out to Jesus, they asked for His pity and mercy. They asked Him to look upon their condition and be moved with compassion to do something to help them. This is also what we do when we find ourselves in difficult situations. We cry out to God for His help because we recognize there is no one else who can deliver and heal us. Sometimes our cry is one of desperation because the pain and the struggles are unbearable. These lepers had come to the end of themselves. They were tired of being outcasts, begging Jesus not to walk by and leave them in their condition. It is fair to conclude they must have heard of His healing of others, so they knew they were not asking an impossible thing. They also knew Him by name, so it is apparent His fame had reached them. Hearing about Him, I wonder if they prayed for Him to come to their region of the world. Whether they asked or not, God had an appointment with their destinies, and Jesus was His answer to their cries.

We must note they did not ask Him specifically to heal them but for pity and mercy. Is it possible that, like many of us, when their opportunity came to be free, they did not ask for what was the most profound need in their hearts? Some have speculated they were asking for financial support, food, and clothing. How often do we also go to Jesus and ask for various things but not necessarily for what we need? Even though the Word tells us to come boldly before the throne of grace and to present our requests to God (Hebrews 4:16), many of us are reluctant to express the greatest need in our hearts to Him. We often hesitate because we are unsure whether He will grant our requests. Sometimes, we hesitate because we feel unworthy to receive anything from Him. Still, some people may feel He is not as concerned about their situations as He is about others' situations.

How many of us can honestly say we have not wondered and questioned why we have not received the answers to many of our prayer requests? We have looked at other people and seen their prosperity, successes, and the manifestation of their healing, yet we are still struggling. When you question God's willingness to heal you, remember He is impartial (Acts 10:34). He is a faithful God, even when we do not understand why some people readily receive their answers and others do not. You will go to a deeper level as you learn to trust Him during these times. You will also develop a more significant relationship.

I have come to understand when I cry to God for help and He does not move, it is not because He does not love me or because He loves me any less than He does others. God is always at work in my heart and life, perfecting the things which concern me. As I wait and wait, I will always ask Him if it is possible to expedite my situation. I continue to hold on even when He does not move when I expect Him to. Why? Because I have put my hope and trust only in Him, and He is my only recourse. The world has nothing to offer me, so if I walk away from God or become luke-warm in my service to Him, it will profit me nothing. However, if I stay connected to Him by holding tightly to His promises, He will always see me through. Many of us, like the lepers, find that Jesus is available, but we forget to ask for the right things. We generally ask for items that are only a temporary fix for our prob-lems. We allow Jesus to pass by us when He is the only one with the power to change our circumstances.

We must ask ourselves if we have been in our situation so long we have become comfortable living in it. Is it possible the lepers had asked for pity and mercy so long it became a habit? Is it also possible that even after recognizing who Jesus was, they asked Him for the same things they asked of other people? I encourage you to remember Jesus is unlike any other person you will ever meet. He has the answers for life, and since eternity is in His hands, so are you and your needs. Jesus, in faithfulness, did not give the lepers what they asked for; He gave them what they needed. Jesus recognized the need for healing was the greatest need they had. In healing their bodies, He also healed their emotional wounds as well as their physical wounds.

When we are traumatized in our bodies, it also affects our

souls. The length of the struggle affects the condition of our souls because some of us will begin to lose hope. When we fall into hopelessness, we lose the desire to fight. I have been around some people who will tell you they are tired and ready to go home to God after a long battle with sickness and disease. Often it is the family members who want to hold on to them. We forget those who belong to Jesus never die. They will live with Him throughout eternity. Since we will miss them, we selfishly hold on because we are not ready to let go. We forget that there is no more sickness or pain in the presence of the Father. For those who have accepted Jesus as Savior, you get to spend eternity—forever and ever with those who also love Him. Remember to make your genuine requests known to God.

Healing In Motion

In Luke 17:14, Jesus gave the lepers one command, "Go and show yourselves to the priests." As they obeyed and started going to the priests, they were healed. They had to do something to obtain their healing, follow the command, and act obediently. If any of them had heard the order and failed to step out on it, they would not have received their healing. Why did Jesus tell them to show themselves to the priests? Only the priests could pronounce a person with leprosy or skin disease as clean or unclean (Leviticus 13). Only the priests could rightly say they were healed of leprosy and allow them back into society.

The word 'show' that Jesus used in His command suggests some things to us. This passage means to cause to be seen or to point out something to someone. Jesus was pointing out to the priests that He had healed the lepers. This was a lesson—a demonstration of His power to them—because many refused to believe He was the Son of God, who had all power and authority in His hands. At no point did Jesus pray and command the lepers to be healed. He implied they would be healed as they went toward the priests. If these lepers had hesitated, questioned why He did not pray for them, or doubted the command, they would have missed their divine time of visitation.

I believe we can sometimes miss our healing because we have programmed ourselves to listen for a specific word or phrase. We may not believe our healing is available if we do not hear these words. This is due in part to how we have been taught. We have limited God and put Him in a box concerning how we will be healed. I have seen people become offended because they did not like how someone was ministered to regarding their healing. They miss the point that even though the method was different, the result was the manifested healing. If you study the life of Jesus, you will see He was just as unorthodox as His Father. He was not limited by man's belief of how He should act or operate. He forged ahead, only doing what God asked Him to do. This should also be our position—to only do what God asks us to do. Remember that God is the only One we must honor and please with our service and devotion.

Some feel only certain people can pray for them to be healed, but the Bible tells us differently. James 5:16 says, "Confess your faults one to another, and pray one for another, that ye may be healed. The effectual fervent prayer of a righteous man availeth much." The requirement for praying and seeing someone healed is you are a righteous person who is fervent when praying for others. This means you pray for them with the same passion and devotion you would use when praying for yourself.

When the lepers asked Jesus for mercy and pity, they probably expected something else from Him, but in His wisdom, Jesus healed them instead. The lepers operated in knowledge and faith by accepting the Words of the Savior and then moved based on what they heard. The result was a transformed life.

As we accept and move out on the words Jesus speaks to our hearts, we will also experience a spectacular move of God in our midst. As we hear the commands and obey them, we are guaranteed success. When Jesus speaks a Word over your life, it has all the power and backing of the God-head. His Word shall not return void to your life but will bring you to the exact thing God has in mind for you. I challenge you not to limit what He can do in you and for you.

One Made Whole

One of the lepers received more remarkable healing than all the others because He recognized who Jesus was. As he walked toward the priests with the other nine lepers, he realized he was healed. He did not continue but turned back to Jesus and began glorifying Him with a loud voice. If he praised Jesus in a loud voice, the others could hear him. They also realized a great miracle had taken place in their bodies, but they continued toward the priests. They did not return to give Jesus worship. Unlike the others, this leper went to Jesus and fell at His feet in worship while expressing his thanks. This one leper recognized that only a greater High Priest could have healed him. Jesus questioned if not all the lepers were healed and why only one came back to say thanks. Then, He said something profound. He gave us the identity of the one who returned; he was a Samaritan. From this distinction, we can conclude the other nine lepers were probably Jews, His chosen people.

The Samaritan leper was a sinner, an outcast who recognized his need for the Savior. He was thankful for his gift and not ashamed to proclaim his appreciation loudly. He was just as loud in praising God as when he had loudly asked for help. His loud praise, exaltation, and thanks did not move the others to join him. They noticed their skins were disease-free but did not cry out to Jesus as they had initially done when they needed healing. They received the miracle but ignored the Miracle Worker. The one leper worshipped Jesus for His power, majesty, and splendor that had been displayed so mightily in his life.

We can learn from this that the ones healed did not think it necessary to thank the One who healed them. They received Jesus' gift and went on their way without acknowledging what they had received. At times, we also forget to say thank you for all Jesus has done for us. We take our healing, miracles, and the blessings of God for granted. Some people may even have an entitlement spirit. They act as if they are owed the help and the blessings they receive. When we have unthankful hearts, we must examine ourselves to see what has gone wrong in our souls. It is a natural response to say thank you when someone has done something for us, no matter how insignificant it may be in our eyes. The mere fact someone would go out of their way to help us is significant. We were not owed the sacrifice of Jesus on the cross, nor did we deserve the help and support we received from others. It is only the grace of God that causes us to receive the blessings we are given.

In my years of doing mission outreaches in the USA and internationally, I have seen such a difference in the levels of people's appreciation. Some people in the USA will not make a concerted effort to come and receive what you are there to give them even though you are literally on their doorsteps. Some do not want to hear the Word of God preached or about the One who sent you. They often come to the event at the very end only to receive the food and the gifts. I have to work on my attitude when this happens and still give them the items. However, I have found such desperation in people in other nations because they do not have the governmental support we have in the USA. They will walk for miles to come and hear the Word and stand and sit in the sun for hours until they receive what little they are given. They are always so grateful for what God has provided and have helped me be more thankful for everything I receive.

What Jesus saw in the Jewish lepers who did not return to thank Him is what He had seen throughout His ministry. Most of the people were self-seeking and self-serving. John 12:37 tells us they were always looking for a sign but were not interested in Jesus or His message. Matthew 23:25 says they looked clean on the outside but were empty on the inside.

The one leper recognized a greater Priest had healed him. Only the genuinely great one could perform such a wondrous miracle. He realized he was in the presence of the great High Priest, the One who was more significant than all other earthly priests combined. This leper did not continue his journey toward the earthly priest but turned back to the One who could give him eternal life. We must also recognize who Jesus is and what He can do. He will do above and beyond what you can even ask Him to do. This leper received something the others did not because he had a revelation and pursued Jesus.

Healing Versus Wholeness

When faced with sickness, most of us will petition God for healing. Some people do not speak to the Lord at any time other than when they are sick or struggling. To experience the healing touch and power of the Lord in our lives is an experience beyond description. The freedom He brings from physical pain also frees us from emotional pain. When we are sick in our bodies, we generally experience emotional torment from the devil. He harasses our minds with worry and anxiety, exacerbating the circumstance. He tells us we are never going to get well and we are going to die. This torment creates such turmoil in our minds and hearts it can adversely affect us just as significantly as the sickness in our bodies.

To experience not only the healing power of Jesus but also to be made whole by Him is an entirely different experience. Let me explain. All ten lepers were healed. This means the spoken words of Jesus stopped the disease that had been ravishing their bodies. Whatever was producing the disease in their bodies was nullified when Jesus sent them to see the priest. The one leper who returned to give thanks experienced something more incredible than healing; he was made whole. Jesus did something extra for this leper. He went beyond just stopping the disease to repairing the damage the disease had caused in his body and his emotions. Remember, leprosy is a disease that attacks the body, destroying mainly the extremities, thus, causing loss of fingers, nose, toes, etc., and leaving people unable to use their limbs effectively. Jesus said to the leper who returned, "Were there not ten cleansed? But where are the nine? There are not found that returned to give glory to God, save this stranger. And he said unto him, Arise, go thy way: thy faith hath made thee whole." (Luke 17:17-19).

To be made whole speaks of salvation, deliverance, and freedom from all diseases and their effects. Jesus not only saved this leper, but He also restored his body to a new state. The parts that were destroyed were restored. Anyone looking at him would not find any evidence his body was once ravaged by leprosy. The other nine, though healed, still carried the evidence they had been lepers. They were not made whole. I, therefore, contend when people saw them, they always had to reassure them they were healed and no longer contagious and were allowed to reenter society. How much better for the one who only had to share his testimony of what Jesus had done? He was no longer looked upon as a leper because all evidence had been erased.

This example reminds me the blood of Jesus erased all evidence of our sins on the cross at Calvary. When the enemy attempts to accuse us, we can remind him the blood of Jesus has completely washed, healed, purified, and made us whole. We no longer wear the scars of our warfare, and He has removed the evidence of the traumas from our lives.

The fighting often matches the warfare in our bodies and minds. Jesus died not only to heal you physically but also to make you completely whole and well in spirit, soul, and body. Your heart and life are now changed, and you can renew your mind daily with the Word of God.

I imagine when the one leper walked away from Jesus after being made whole, he was beyond amazed by the power and glory of God. He had no idea when he returned to say thank you that, he would experience the level of deliverance and freedom this miracle brought to his life. Can you imagine his testimony not only to his family but also to everyone who previously knew he had leprosy? His testimony was powerful and convicting to the other nine lepers who did not return to give thanks. When the hand of God touches your life, you will be forever changed. When He heals your body and frees you from worry and anxiety, He sets you on a journey of living the abundant life Jesus died to give you.

Lessons To Live By

- We must have a Christ-centered life.
- Always give thanks to God.
- Our praise and worship to God must equal our requests for His help.
- Give thanks in everything, not for the troubles, but because God is with us to see us through them.
- We are commissioned to help the helpless even when they are unthankful.
- God does not limit His gifts only to believers. He came to seek and save the lost.
- Do not discriminate against people because of their religion, or lack thereof, because God can change a heart.
- Everyone we meet needs a relationship with Jesus; we are His instruments on earth.
- Let your life reflect your thankfulness and appreciation for all God has done.

A Scripture for Healing – Proverbs 4:20-23

Father, thank You that Proverbs 4:20-23 tells me that as I listen to Your words, and keep them before my eyes and do not allow them to depart from my heart, they will bring life to me and health to all of my flesh. It reminds me to keep my heart with all diligence, for out of it are the issues of life. Father, help me to keep my heart secure and safe in You so I will experience Your healing not only in my body but also in my emotions, in Jesus' name.
Amen!

Jesus, Have Mercy on Me

⤜∾⤛

Have you ever felt so emotionally wounded you cried out to God for mercy? You were in desperate need of His help because the pain and struggles in your life were more than you could bear. I have been there. But greater than my pain is the pain of others who, in desperation, also cried out for mercy. I cannot recount the times I have listened, counseled, or prayed for someone desperate for God to intervene on their behalf.

The emotional scars or wounds people have suffered and are suffering are sometimes unbearable. I have listened to numerous stories of abuse and wondered how the person survived to tell their story.

A close and dear friend recounted her desperate cry to God: "God, will I ever be happy? Will I ever meet someone who loves and does not abuse me?" When you hear her story, you will understand this desperate cry to God, even though, at the time, she did not have a relationship with Him and had no knowledge of God's precious Son, Jesus. She shared that even though she did not know God personally, she was fully aware He existed. When the father of her children abused her, she would find solace in believing God would one day come to her rescue.

One of the most horrific incidents in her life was when her husband slammed her head against a wall because she had not cooked his eggs the way he liked them. Her head had been banged against a wall many times, which resulted in a small mass on her brain that the doctors regularly monitor to ensure it is not growing. This is only one horrendous example of the many times she has cried for mercy. She also sought after the mercies of God in her childhood because she came out of tremendous abuse.

Sadly, people who have had an abusive childhood often end up in abusive relationships. They have not seen a healthy home environment, so they are unaware of what a healthy person looks like when they meet one. Therefore, they are instinctively drawn to people with a propensity to abuse them. This is what is known as dealing with a familiar spirit.

Let me cite an example of what a familiar spirit is. Have you ever known anyone in an unhealthy relationship who lived in a particular city, and when they moved to a different city, they ended up in another abusive relationship with someone who had similar qualities to the person they left? This example describes some people with whom I have spoken. This familiar spirit attached itself to them, even though they were in a new location because it was familiar with their history and the way they had always lived.

You cannot outrun or change your past, but you can decide you have had enough of the enemy's attacks and change what you attract to your life by changing your beliefs about yourself. Remember, God created you in His image and likeness. He is the only one who knows the significant deposits He has made in you that can make you into the phenomenal person He birthed you to be.

Today, my friend who had an abusive spouse is a person full of joy and peace because of her relationship with Jesus Christ. Nothing worries her or shakes her confidence in God. My friend has unbelievable faith, trust, and hope in God's faithfulness. The damage the enemy intended to do in her life was unsuccessful because she entered a relationship with Christ. Since Jesus changed her life, my friend no longer settles for less than what He has for her. Today she is in a healthy, thriving marriage where God has center stage, and He is doing wonderful things in their lives as a couple. My friend has not allowed the wounds and scars of her past to keep her in bondage. What the enemy meant for evil in her life, she is using it for the glory of God and to set others free. Our great and merciful Savior heard her cries for mercy and responded with love and compassion by setting her free.

The word 'mercy' resonates with compassion for those drowning in sorrow and distress. Psalm 20:1-4 says, "May the Lord answer you when you are in distress; may the name of the God of Jacob protect you. May he send you help from the sanctuary and grant you support from Zion. May he remember all your sacrifices and accept your burnt offerings. May he give you the desire of your heart and make all your plans succeed." God is undoubtedly concerned about your troubles and distress. He makes it clear in the scriptures He will answer you, protect you, send you help, remember all you have sacrificed for Him, and grant you the desires of your heart.

Since He cannot lie, there is absolutely no way you will not be reimbursed for every season of struggle you have endured. This is the reason we always win. God ensures our victory when the enemy tries to destroy us emotionally, physically, or spiritually. We may go through many battles, but with His help, we will always win the war in the end.

Proverbs 6:31 says when a thief is caught; he has to return seven-fold, even if it costs him his household. What has the enemy stolen from you—your health, finances, marriage, or children? As a child of God, you have the right to demand he reimburse you for all your losses. Demand he returns seven-fold to your life because that's what God's Word promises.

The word mercy is used approximately two hundred and seventy-six times in the Bible, which tells us God's compassion toward us is unending. The word mercy means to be compassionate and to have forbearance, and it is God's loyalty and devotion to the promises that are in His Word. The term mercy is most often used when describing God, but Spirit-filled, born-again Christians can and should also operate in this gift of mercy. Often, mercy can be translated as kindness or steadfast love. Many times in the Bible, we find the word 'loving-kindness,' which describes God's mercy and His attitude toward us.

For centuries, people have pleaded for God to have mercy on them. They have asked for His help when they realize they are overtaken with trouble without Him. Lamentations 3:22-26 is a powerful scripture. It is a heartfelt tribute to our loving God, who has the power to bring help and healing in the depth of our crises. It says, "Because of the Lord's great love, we are not consumed, for his compassions never fail. They are new every morning; great is your faithfulness. I say, 'The Lord is my portion; therefore, I will wait for him." The Lord is good to those whose hope is in him, to the one who seeks him; it is good to wait quietly for the salvation of the Lord."

There are seven great promises in these verses. Let's look closely at what He is saying to us:

1. His love keeps us from being consumed with the difficulties of life.
2. His compassions toward us never fail. This tells us His compassions are many, not just one.
3. Each morning, we are renewed with His compassions.
4. His faithfulness toward us is great.

5. He is our portion—our share, due, and our destiny.
6. The Lord is good to those who hope in Him.
7. He will save us as we wait quietly for Him.

Such promises should ignite your heart with confident assurance that God will always be merciful to those who cry out to Him. So in your distress, cry out to Him. He will come to your rescue when there is turmoil in your mind and emotions. When hopelessness tries to set in, remember He is always available. He is a very present help in times of trouble (Psalm 46:1). I encourage you to seek after Him when you are in trouble and pursue Him when things are going well in your life. Therefore, you will immediately know what to do when trouble comes (it is not if it comes but when because the enemy will ensure that those who love the Lord encounter difficulties). Call upon the name of the Lord. He will hear, and He will answer you!

Jesus Is Listening

The story of blind Bartimaeus recorded in Luke 18:35-43 resounds with the mercy, love, and favor of our Lord and Savior. We can glean some profound truths and insights from how Jesus responded to this man who cried out for His help. Within the cry was an understanding that the One passing by had the power to heal and transform lives. Before meeting Bartimaeus (we will call him Bart), Jesus had healed ten lepers, talked about the second coming, met and ministered to the rich young ruler, and shared a parable about prayer. After completing these assignments, He headed to Jerusalem via Jericho. I believe God mapped out each step Jesus took, connecting Him with every person God wanted to heal, deliver, and set free. In each of these lives, we see the power of

God at work, and the people experience significant change. Their stories give us an amazing view of what God can do when we are yielded and submitted to Him.

As Jesus approached Jericho, a blind man was sitting by the roadside begging. When he heard the crowd going by, he asked what was happening. They told him, "Jesus of Nazareth is passing by." He called out, "Jesus Son of David, have mercy on me!" Those who led the way rebuked him and told him to be quiet, but he shouted all the more, "Son of David, have mercy on me!" Jesus stopped and ordered the man be brought to him. When he came near, Jesus asked him, "What do you want me to do for you?" "Lord, I want to see," he replied. Jesus said to him, "Receive your sight; your faith has healed you." Immediately he received his sight and followed Jesus, praising God. When all the people saw it, they also praised God.
Luke 18:34-43 (NIV)

Of the many people Jesus healed, blind Bartimaeus is one of the few whose name we are given. It is evident he had some knowledge of Jesus as Messiah because he addressed Him as the Son of David. Because Bartimaeus recognized Jesus as his Savior, he was not hesitant to call on Him for help. He knew Jesus was capable of healing him. Bart was in the right place at the right time, and as a result, the power of Jesus changed him. Jesus encountered Bart along the route He took to travel to Jerusalem. Bart was sitting by the roadside, begging for financial help to sustain himself. Bart heard a crowd passing by and began to inquire about what was happening.

We must not become complacent in our struggles to not miss Jesus and His blessings in our lives. Sometimes, unlike Bart, we have sat by the side of the road so long we no longer inquire about what is happening around us. We no longer seek answers because we have become stuck in our daily routines or struggles. We get up and do the same thing daily, not expecting anything spectacular to happen to us.

Imagine with me Bart had been by the side of the road for years. It is probably reasonable to conclude that this was his daily routine except for the Sabbath, Saturday. He came to that spot daily because this was where he received his support. After many years of sitting by the road, it probably never dawned on him he would one day encounter the One who would set him free. This day was probably like any other day in his life. But on this day, God had made an assignment to connect with Bart and use his life as a forever testimony to God's power and mercy. I want you to see that even though God had made the assignment, Bart had to participate in the plan to get his miracle. It is safe to say there were others by the side of the road that day who were probably as downtrodden in life as Bart. However, they did not inquire about what was happening and missed out on their miracle.

The scripture says Bart heard the crowd going by and asked what was happening. Because of the miracles and the messages Jesus taught, He developed a considerable following. In this instance, there was a crowd of people following Jesus, and their movements and the excitement in the atmosphere were loud enough to cause a person who was blind to realize something different was happening around him. When the people told Bart Jesus of Nazareth was passing by, he did not hesitate and instantly cried out for help. Apparently, he had heard about Jesus and the miracles He had been performing. The fame of Jesus had reached Jericho, and it is evident since most of Bart's time was spent by the side of the road, he had heard the stories. This was his chance for a changed life.

For many years, people who felt sorry for Bart had taken care of him. He could have stayed in that condition and continued to receive the handouts, but he wanted more out of life. He was not satisfied to remain in the same situation he was in for the rest of his life.

Unlike blind Bartimaeus, some people have accepted the desperate conditions life has dealt them. Some are unwilling to reach out for something beyond what they currently have. They have been in their struggles for so long that they have become hopeless and helpless. Amid their hopelessness, they do not strive for anything different. They believe this is their lot in life and have lost the will to fight for a different outcome. Even though Bart had probably been in this situation since birth, he had not lost his will to fight. He wanted a different outcome, and when his opportunity came, he seized it with all his might.

Recognizing it was Jesus, the Healer, who was passing by, Bart cried out for His help. The crowd was probably noisy, so Jesus might not have heard him, although I believe Jesus did hear him. He is the Son of God and can see and hear beyond what you and I can comprehend. I think God wanted to see how determined Bart was to obtain his miracle. Would he give up after the first cry when he did not get a response, or would Bart keep calling until he got an answer? Bart began to cry louder. He could not run to Jesus because he could not see. So he used what he had—his voice—to get the attention he needed. His cry for help was very loud because the people told him to quiet down. However, he ignored them and cried out even louder. He was not going to miss his one opportunity to receive his healing. Bart not only called Jesus by His name, but he called Him the Son of David. This was a man who knew the Law and understood who Jesus was. Jesus is indeed the Son of David whom God had promised to send to bring deliverance to His people, and Bart recognized this. In calling Jesus the Son of David, Bart realized the Savior of the world had come and was close to him.

The Bible said Jesus stopped. He heard the voice of a man who recognized who He was, who called Him by His proper title, and Jesus responded to the cry. Not only did Jesus stop, but He also commanded them to bring Bart to Him. He did not merely ask or suggest they bring him; He commanded them to do so. The word command is a strong word and means Jesus demanded, ordered, called, or gave an implicit order he be brought to Him. Jesus made it clear an audience with this blind man was mandatory.

Imagine the joy in Bart's heart when he heard footsteps heading toward him and heard the words the master wanted to see him. Mark 10:50 says he threw off his coat before running to the Master. This is significant because his coat signified he had permission from the authorities to sit and beg for help since he was disabled and needed support. By taking off and leaving his coat, he said, "I am done with this lifestyle of begging, and from this moment on, I will not need the financial help of others." This was a powerful act of faith and confidence from a man who had probably spent his life begging by the roadside. This act said to Jesus, and everyone watching he expected to walk away from his encounter with Jesus healed and free. He would no longer be the needy person he had been. He would be able to support himself and become a giver in society and no longer a taker.

Conversely, if Bart had not acted with that level of faith and had not accepted the help of the people Jesus sent to him, I believe the outcome could have been different. What I see taking place in this scripture is a test. Bart had cried loudly for help, and when help came, he had to decide to move toward it. He could have said, "I am blind. Why did Jesus not come to me Himself?" Jesus did not do this because He recognized Bart had to be a participant in his miracle. Bart had to do something to get the results he wanted.

We can sometimes develop a bad attitude when things do not work out how we hoped and prayed they would. I can attest to this, and I know others can as well. We cry, pray, and ask for Jesus' help, but when He sends it, we do not appreciate how the answer came, how it was packaged, and who delivered it. Therefore, we can develop a bad attitude instead of being thankful.

Bart did not care about what he had to do to get his miracle. He recognized his blessing had come, and he needed the help of others to get the final result. I am sure his act of faith impacted many people. The blind man left his coat and all the opportunities and the provisions it held. If he ever needed the coat again, he probably would not find it because chances are someone else grabbed hold of it, knowing its benefits. There was no going back for Bart.

An Audience With The Savior

Bart is now standing before the Master. He could not see Him. He probably had never heard His voice before, yet, he knew it was Jesus. When Jesus made the command and His people obeyed, Bart was sure he was standing before his merciful Savior, the one who could help him. Jesus did not assume Bart wanted to be healed; He asked him what he wanted. It is reasonable to conclude Bart was making all the commotion because he wished to be healed. However, Jesus asked Bart to articulate what he wanted. His cry could have meant he wanted financial help, but he told Jesus he wanted to see. Jesus gave him what he asked for and told him his faith had saved him. His faith had not healed him but saved him. I believe Jesus gave Bart something more significant than he expected. He saved him. Remember, the word saved in Greek is Sozo, which means to heal, save, deliver, and set free. Jesus opened Bart's eyes. He saved him and gave him a place in eternity. He set him free from all the years of oppression and set him free to live a life that glorified God and brought joy to Bart's heart.

In our emotional and physical struggles, we can sometimes become depressed by the condition in which we find ourselves. From Bart's perspective, he had been a beggar for years and had to depend on others to help him. I am sure he felt degraded in this needy position. Jesus, who understands us, knew the emotional turmoil Bart had endured and went beyond his physical healing to provide emotional healing. Jesus saw beyond the request for sight. He heard the desperation in Bart's cries because he ignored the people who tried to quiet him down and cried louder. The cry was a plea to be freed from his bondage and live a normal life. I will venture to say this is probably not the only time Bart cried out to God for help. He probably asked for help throughout his life, and God purposefully sent Jesus through Jericho to answer Bart's cries.

How many times or years have you cried out for help while in the pit of despair or depression? At times you may have asked, "God are You listening? Can You please help me?" The same God who heard Bart's cries and sent Jesus to deliver him is the same One who also hears your cries for help. God is willing and available to help you. Do not give up if He does not answer right away. You must continue to petition Him until your answer comes. I do not believe the compassionate and merciful Savior we serve will withhold a response, even though we may have to wait for it. Even when the answer is delayed, He is not saying no to your cry. He is saying, "Hold on. I am coming, and my reward is with Me." I encourage you to remember the Word says His compassions never fail, and His mercy endures forever. He is your merciful Savior.

Lessons To Live By

- God always hears your cries for help.
- In your distress, God will respond.
- Though the answers may be delayed, do not give up.
- Amid hopelessness, continue to hope in God. He will never fail you.
- When others want you to be quiet, cry louder. They do not understand your struggles.
- When Jesus sends help, do not miss your opportunity just because it came in a way that was different from what you expected.
- The compassion of Jesus never fails.
- His mercy endures through all generations.
- You may only ask for one thing, but Jesus knows everything and will do exceedingly and abundantly above what you ask of Him.

A Scripture for Healing – Psalm 103:1-5

Father, thank You that Your Word tells me to bless the Lord, O my soul, and to let all that is within me bless Your holy name. It also tells me I must not forget Your benefits as I bless You. Thank You for forgiving me and for healing all my diseases. I also thank You for redeeming my life from destruction and giving me Your loving-kindness and tender mercies. I thank You for satisfying my mouth with good things, so my youth is renewed like the eagles. Thank You for Your promises in this scripture and help me begin to enjoy the benefits of belonging to You, in Jesus' name.
Amen!

From Unbelief to Believing

C an you remember operating in unbelief even though you knew God kept His promises? As we look over our lives, I believe many of us can remember the many times we doubted the outcome of our situation would be favorable.

Most people tend to lean more toward a negative mindset than a positive one. There is a deep-seated fear in our souls that our struggles will never end and the blessings will never come.

The longer we wait for the manifestation, the greater the fear we will not receive the desired results. Despite our praying and standing in faith, we are still challenged to believe we can win over the difficult situations in life. We declare the Word but get despondent when we don't see immediate changes in our health, financial problems, families, or jobs. We want to know why God has not moved when we have prayed diligently.

Some of us feel God has not freed us because something in our lives displeases Him and causes Him not to favor us. Let me tell you clearly; God does not punish His children; He does discipline us for our good. He is not a mean or harsh Father. No wrongdoing can ever change the deep love, devotion, and compassion flowing from the Father's heart toward you.

As I study the Bible, I am encouraged to see the many men and women with significant character flaws, yet God used them powerfully. Let's look at a few examples so we can be encouraged if God could turn their lives around and then use them; He can do the same for us. Adam and Eve disobeyed God and caused spiritual death for all people after that. Cain killed Abel, yet God defended Him and challenged anyone who tried to harm Him. Abraham lied about his wife Sarah being his sister. He also stepped out of God's plan for producing a son of promise and had Ishmael with his slave girl. Jacob plotted with his mother to steal his brother Esau's birthright, then disappeared for years to avoid retribution. Joseph was boastful about the dreams God gave him, so his brothers became jealous and sold him into slavery, even though they initially wanted to kill him. Moses was a murderer who fled imprisonment, but God later used him to deliver His chosen people. These examples show us mankind has tremendous moral challenges, yet our faithful God has the power to redeem us, set us free, and then use us for His glory.

Our struggles with unbelief stem from our uncertainty that God will respond favorably toward us. The longer we struggle, the deeper our uncertainty and fear we will ever attain the things we so desire. In our ministry to the poor and the less privileged in society, we have found the most challenging thing we do is to convince people their situation can change for the better. Some people have lived in such deplorable conditions for so long that it is hard for them to believe things can change. If we cannot change their beliefs, the changes they greatly desire will become impossible.

We all need a reason to hope, and our hope is tied to what we believe. We need something positive to look forward to, which will keep us from giving up and persevering to the end. I understand the struggles to keep believing and hoping when the journey has been paved with difficulties. Sometimes, you must dig your heels in and decide it does not matter what it looks like in the natural; God has the final say about the outcome.

Unbelief will rob you of your peace and keep you in the pit of despair. A great deal of warfare goes on in our minds as we try to hold on to our faith confessions. We have to battle to stay at peace, and we also fight to stay out of depression or to keep depressive thoughts at bay. You, at times, must repeatedly say, "God will bring me through, and He will give me the right outcome, in Jesus' name."

Unbelief will keep us in a negative cycle that is difficult to break. In my years of praying and encouraging others, I have heard their desperation as they respond with, "What if it is cancer? What if I don't survive this trouble?" Their cry is a plea for comfort and reassurance God will hear and respond to them during their crisis. Although we can provide comfort, it still comes down to the person deciding. God can be trusted no matter the outcome.

There is no way you or I can pour our faith into people's hearts because we are not the ones facing the difficulties. Each person must find mustard seed faith to believe for themselves. When no one else is available to talk to late in the midnight hours, God is always there, ready, and willing to listen. Although people will stand in the gap for us, we cannot survive and overcome based on their beliefs or faith.

Some of us may wish we had the faith we see operating in others. Some people simply believe in God. They see the problems in front of them, but their view is not clouded by what they see. In their opinion, God is more significant than anything they are facing. Many of us strive to get to this place of faith and rest in God's faithfulness. The Bible gives us many examples of people of great faith, and we can learn from them how to go from unbelief to believing it will also be well with us.

In John 4, we find a stellar example of someone who simply

took Jesus at His Word and believed despite the devastating circumstances. As you journey with me through his story, ask the Holy Spirit to help you apply it to your situation.

When they entered Galilee, the Galileans welcomed Him because
they had seen everything He did in Jerusalem during the festival.
For they also had gone to the festival. Then He went again to Cana
of Galilee, where He had turned the water into wine. There was a
particular royal official whose son was ill at Capernaum. When this
man heard Jesus had come from Judea into Galilee, he went to Him
and pleaded with Him to come down and heal his son, for he was
about to die.
John 4:45-47 (HCSB)

Let me set the stage for this story by looking at the previous chapter. Jesus had been in Samaria, where He freed the Samaritan woman at the well. He was initially on His way to Galilee when He made this stop. The usual route to get to Galilee was by way of the Jordan Valley. However, Jesus went in a different direction to connect with this woman and heal and make her whole. From this, you can infer Jesus is willing to be inconvenienced to bring healing to people's lives. Once the Samaritan woman and her entire town were converted, He continued His journey to Galilee. Jesus undertook this trip to Galilee one year after performing His first miracle of turning water into wine. The miracle He would perform for this nobleman's son was His second miracle in Cana of Galilee.

The first person to meet Jesus upon His arrival was this unbelieving nobleman. He did not yet believe Jesus was Christ, the Son of God, but he believed in the miracles Jesus had performed.

A challenging situation in our lives will often drive many of us to Jesus, whether we believe in Him. Others will pull away from Him because they may blame Him for their troubles. However, when He touches and changes our situations, this opens our hearts wider to His saving power.

That is what happened to this man. The nobleman was one of Herod's officials who lived in Capernaum. What you must see in this miracle is Jesus healed the son of a man who served Herod. Two years after this miracle, Herod sent Jesus to His crucifixion. Jesus, being God, and having all knowledge, was fully aware of this, yet, He did not discriminate nor hesitate to help this man. We must follow His example of helping others even when we think they are undeserving of our help. Although people might treat us unjustly, we must not withhold the love and compassion of Jesus from them.

Capernaum was approximately fifteen miles from Cana of Galilee; therefore, the nobleman had traveled for about five hours on foot or by horseback to connect to Jesus. He was desperate for a miracle and was willing to do whatever was necessary to ensure he received it. Since this man had such a high-ranking position, we can conclude he had taken his son to the best physicians without success. Therefore, Jesus was his last hope.

For a moment, let us walk in this nobleman's shoes. He made the long journey to meet the Miracle Worker he had not personally encountered before. The nobleman probably does not yet believe Jesus' claim to be the Messiah. With each tedious step along the way, I am sure negative thoughts bombarded his mind—he might be wasting his time and the time he was expending to see Jesus could be better spent with his dying son. Like most of us, he probably battled the 'what if' thoughts. What if his son died while he was away? What if, in the son's dying moments, he asked to see his father, who was not there? What if before he gets to Jesus' word comes, his son has died? Step by step, he thought of his son, whose life hung in the balance. Step by step, the nobleman had to battle unbelief and hold on to the hope something good would come of his decision to meet with Jesus. Are you getting the picture?

What are your 'what ifs?' You can believe Jesus is only steps away from giving you a miracle.

This man's desperation to see his son healed was the driving force that kept him moving toward his miracle. Although it would take many hours to get to Jesus and then return home, it did not matter because his situation required desperate measures. There are things we have faced or will face that may require us to take some desperate measures to receive our reward. Even though each step of the journey is agonizing, our hope in the One we serve keeps us pressing on.

This nobleman did not yet believe in Jesus, but he made the journey. He believed in the miracles he heard but had not yet developed faith in the Miracle Worker. He did not waver in unbelief about receiving his blessing. He must have concluded in his heart his request would be granted. It's the only logical reason to undertake such a journey.

Consider why this man would have faith in the journey. Is it possible he knew someone who had received a miracle from Jesus? Even though he did not yet know the Savior, he must have reasoned a person who would take time to meet the needs of the less fortunate must be someone who had a great love for people. His faith in what he heard was steady and secure.

I am reminded of 1 Corinthians 15:58 when thinking about the nobleman's tenacity. It says, "Therefore, my dear brothers, stand firm. Let nothing move you. Always give yourselves fully to the work of the Lord because you know your labor in the Lord is not in vain." Doubt did not move the nobleman from his decision. Fear and uncertainty could not stop him. He was immovable and believed his labor of love for his son would not be in vain. Jesus would come through for him.

Nobleman Meets Jesus

As you delve deeper into this story, you will see Jesus is available even to those who do not acknowledge Him as Lord. The nobleman had concluded his journey and was now in the presence of Jesus. Let us listen in on the conversation that led to his miracle.

When this man heard Jesus had arrived in Galilee from Judea, he went to him and begged him to come and heal his son, who was close to death. "Unless you people see signs and wonders," Jesus told him, "you will never believe." The royal official said, "Sir, come down before my child dies." Jesus replied, "Go. Your son will live." The man took Jesus at his word and departed.
John 4:47-50 (NIV)

The nobleman begged Jesus for the healing of his son, but Jesus' response to him was not welcoming. Jesus did not answer him directly, and His response did not appear to be filled with His usual compassion. He said, "Unless you people see miraculous signs and wonders, you will not believe." Let's unpack what Jesus is saying here. It appears Jesus may have been slightly irritated, yet another person was tugging at Him but not because they desired to know God.

He came to introduce people to the Father, but many people did not receive His gift. His assignment was to turn people back to God by inviting them to denounce their wicked ways. Yet, many clamored only to see more and more miracles.

Jesus sounds weary in the text, but He still responds to the man. What is most interesting in this story is the man did not take offense at Jesus' words, and he ignored the rebuke and stayed intent on his purpose for coming to see Jesus. He reiterated his request, "Sir, come before my son dies." In this dialogue, the nobleman did not address Jesus by name or by His title of Savior or Messiah, and he was respectful and addressed Him as Sir because that was all he knew. Jesus responded his son would live.

Remember, in Chapter 5, I shared the story about the Centurion who sent some Jewish men to Jesus to ask for healing for his servant. In contrasting these two miracles, we see this man did not send his servants or friends to Jesus; he went himself. He was not seeking a miracle for a beloved servant but a beloved son.

The difference between the two stories is the Centurion loved his servant *like a son*, but the nobleman was a father who *loved his son*. No one could undertake this task with the same passion and devotion as this father who was worried about losing his son. No one else could communicate this father's desperation to Jesus but the father. If he had sent someone else when Jesus gave the rebuke, the person might have gotten offended and not continued to press Jesus for help. This father had experienced the hopelessness associated with seeing his son suffer and being helpless to change his situation. He was the most qualified person to speak to Jesus.

Think about some of your struggles. Could anyone communicate your needs to those who helped you the way you did? Could they have poured out your desperation to Jesus the way you did? No one can express our anguish or sorrows to Jesus as we can.

How grateful I am we have access to a Father who listens to the cries and pleas of His children. He does not turn a deaf ear to our requests, even though we may only seek Him with urgency when faced with a devastating crisis. Aren't you glad God is faithful to us even when we are unfaithful to Him? Can you imagine what life would be like if Jesus was as inconsistent in His devotion to us as we have been to Him? Our lives would be filled with the devastation from which many of us would never recover. But He always remains faithful. He is always waiting for His prodigal son or daughter to return home and welcomes us with open arms.

Jesus' response to both these high-ranking men was different. He was ready and willing to go to the Centurion's home; He did not suggest going with his father. He simply gave the Word. I do not believe Jesus had any less compassion for the nobleman's son. As with the Centurion, Jesus recognized this man had faith to believe what he was told. The nobleman also had servants under him who received and carried out his orders. The man heard the words of Jesus, believed them, and turned away to begin his journey home.

The Nobleman's Return Journey

Since we examined the nobleman's journey to meet with Jesus, let us also look at his journey home after hearing Jesus' words. When Jesus said, "Go your way, your son lives," he had to decide to believe the words. Notice that Jesus did not ask his son's name or even what his illness was. He also did not pray with the man for healing; Jesus simply spoke the words, which was sufficient. Remember, this man was an unbeliever and not yet a follower of Jesus. He was at a crossroads and needed to choose whether or not to step out in absolute faith. He had heard about the other miracles but had to trust Jesus would be open to helping someone who had not yet given his allegiance to Him. He chose correctly and believed the words of the Savior. Armed with these words, he began his journey home.

I believe this man is probably like many of us as it relates to trusting the words of the Savior. We hear and receive them, but we also have to walk them out by faith. The nobleman had a fifteen-mile journey home to meditate on the words of Jesus and to consider whether his son lived or not. In that century, there were no cell phones, emails, or texting, so he had no way of checking if the healing had manifested. I believe the enemy probably tried his best to dissuade this man from trusting Jesus. He had to battle doubt and unbelief. Even though he did not know Jesus personally, he also had to hold tightly to his faith and reason within himself. Jesus was a person of His word. Step by step, this unbelieving nobleman had to acknowledge and accept Jesus had the power to speak words of healing. Even at a distance, those words would come to pass. This nobleman must have wondered if Jesus had ever healed anyone who was not in His immediate presence before, yet he believed.

I can imagine the dialogue that must have taken place in this man's mind was probably the same dialogue you and I had when we were faced with the choice of believing or not believing. Many have had seasons in their lives when they have had to take Jesus at His word. We completely believed His death on the cross provided us with eternal life. We also believed we were forgiven when we confessed our sins and turned our lives over to Him. In the same way, we must learn to trust the promises He has spoken to our hearts will also come to pass.

Since the nobleman was not yet a believer in Jesus, what caused him to believe he had received his miracle? When many of us are in desperate situations, we often come to the end of ourselves and our abilities. Most people will turn to the only One who has the solution. This man was desperate and had found his way to Jesus. I am sure the testimonies he heard assured him Jesus was genuine; therefore, he had hope for what was possible. Determination and desperation were the driving forces. Since he had tried to secure healing for his son through the efforts of others without success, his only hope was the Miracle Worker.

Before Jesus appeared on the scene, no one had performed miracles, healed people, or brought deliverance to the oppressed.

Since the death of the last prophet, Malachi, heaven had been shut up for four hundred years, and the Jews had had no direct word from God during all those years.

The nobleman held on to the words of Jesus and kept them in his heart as he journeyed home. Those words became life to him. The healing was in the spoken words, which held the nobleman steady as he made the long journey home.

Psalm 107:20 says, "He sent His word and healed them, snatching them from the door of death." What do you believe? Is it healing, a job, a family member, a spouse, or the purposes of God for your life? Can you accept the words Jesus has spoken to your heart are pregnant with life-giving provisions? He would not have said them if He did not have the desire or the power to perform them. Even though you cannot see Him as people did centuries ago, His words are still as powerful today as when He walked the earth.

Psalm 138:2 says He has placed His word above His name. Since He has placed His word above His powerful name, you are assured they will be fulfilled in your life. The Bible tells us heaven and earth will pass away, but His word will never pass away (Matthew 24:35). These scriptures reveal how powerful the Word of God is. Like the nobleman, you can hold tightly to His word because He will faithfully bring every single one to pass in your life.

From Unbelief to Believing

When the nobleman went to see Jesus, he was not seeking salvation; therefore, his faith was not 'saving faith;' it was faith for what he needed. This man was not looking for a Savior but a healer.

The nobleman told his family and servants about his decision to pursue Jesus for a miracle. John 4:51 tells us while he was still on the way, his servants met him with the news his son was alive. This would indicate they were aware of his journey since they knew where to look for him to share the good news.

This is an excellent example of training others to believe in the power of Jesus. Not only was he looking for a miracle, but everyone around him was also looking for it. Therefore, when Jesus healed this young boy, many people became aware all power was in Jesus. He alone could heal and deliver those sick or oppressed, which opened their hearts to receive Him.

Consider the excitement and joy that filled home when the young boy got up from his sick bed wholly healed. They watched for their master and could not wait to share this wonderful news with him. Look closely at the master's response, and you will see a change in his heart on the journey home.

When the master heard his son was healed, he did not jump up and down with excitement, although we can be assured he was utterly ecstatic. John 4:52 says he inquired when his son was made well, and they told him it took place the previous day at the seventh hour. The father realized the healing took place at the exact moment Jesus had spoken the words.

While he journeyed home, he had an opportunity to examine his life in light of the words Jesus had spoken about people who only wanted to see signs and miracles. It is sad to say, but many people only pursue Jesus for what they can receive from Him. Their pursuit is not to know Him and to serve Him with whole-hearted devotion but to receive a blessing. Unfortunately, many of these people will return to their old lifestyles and forget what He has done for them.

A few years ago, I experienced one of God's great miracles. We were on a mission trip to Marcala, Honduras. While there, one of our faithful team members received word her sister was gravely ill and in a coma in a hospital back home. They did not have much hope for her survival, and we gathered around her and prayed God would raise her.

This faithful member decided God was not surprised by this sickness, and God was in charge of the outcome since He allowed it during the mission trip. She was allowed to return home but chose to remain and finish her assignment. Upon arriving home, she went directly to the hospital and spent the night there praying and petitioning God for her sister.

The next day, along with two members of my Board of Directors, we went to the hospital to pray for the sister because her situation was grave. We met the husband and a few distraught friends. Looking at this lady hooked to all the medical equipment, we realized if she survived, it would only be by God's grace alone. We anointed her and prayed over her. As I concluded the prayer, I heard the Lord say, "You shall not die but live to declare the works of the Lord" (Psalm 118:17), so I whispered these words directly into her ear.

We spoke to her husband and shared God's love and compassion with him. We also asked if he had a relationship with Jesus, and his response was although he was once saved, he had not remained committed to his faith nor attended church in a very long time. He recommitted his heart to the Lord, and we left the hospital believing God would honor our team member and heal her sister. A few days later, God brought her out of the coma, to the surprise of the family, doctors, and nurses. The power of Jesus healed this woman, and she went back to work a few weeks later. What a wonderful Savior we serve.

In the months following, I checked to see if the husband had kept his word and, along with his wife, gone back to church. Sadly, they had not. About a year later, this team member had surgery, and we went to the hospital to visit her. Her sister was in the room with her, but I did not recognize her. Someone reminded me she was the one God had healed. She was completely healthy with no lingering effects from her trauma, yet, she had not committed her life to Christ. We continue to pray for their salvation and hope it will not take another crisis to lead them to the Savior. Unfortunately, many people pursue Jesus, and when He meets them at the point of their greatest need and brings healing, they still do not decide to serve Him.

I am so glad for this Biblical example of the nobleman. The Bible says he and his entire household believed in Jesus upon hearing the news of his son's healing. When he heard the hour his son was healed, he did not pretend anyone but Jesus had performed this miracle. He did not allow the enemy to convince him his son's sickness was not as bad as it had appeared. The enemy is very good at convincing us not to give proper acknowledgment and thanks for what Jesus has done. This man did not ask about anything other than what Jesus had done. He was more interested in Jesus than in the details of the actual miracle. I wonder if he would have still believed in Him if the miracle had not manifested when Jesus spoke it.

We often expect Jesus to move within our schedule, but His timing is much different from ours. Jesus knew it was vital this miracle be performed on the day and at the exact time of the request, so this man and his family would believe in Him. They believed because of the miracle. They came to 'saving faith' because Jesus reached into their lives and touched and healed someone dear to them. They believed not only because of what they heard but also because of what they saw. Many of us have to believe before we receive the manifestation, which is what faith is all about.

As I conclude this chapter, I want you to ask yourself some questions. When do you take Jesus at His word? Are you waiting for the manifestation before you believe? How willing are you to fully trust Jesus and take Him at His word? Do you see your situation as much bigger than Jesus? Will Jesus respond to your cries for help? These critical questions and your responses will help you be ready when the enemy comes against you. You can be assured Jesus has the answers, and when He speaks the Word over your situation, your victory is assured. You can rely on Jesus, and He always keeps His Word.

Do you believe? **I BELIEVE!**

Lessons To Live By

- Unbelievers will also experience the miracle-working power of Jesus.
- The words of Jesus have the power to heal even at a distance.
- We must not only seek Jesus for miracles but also salvation.
- We have to persevere to receive our miracles.
- If you are desperate to connect with Jesus, you will connect with Him.
- When Jesus speaks, we must take Him at His word.
- We must activate our faith to receive our miracles.
- Miracles will bring unbelievers to faith in Jesus.

A Scripture For Healing – Jeremiah 30:17

Father, thank You for Your promise to restore health to me and to heal me of my wounds. I believe Your words and trust You to do just what you say. Therefore today, as an act of faith, I declare I am healed in Jesus' name.

Amen!

Rise and Be Healed

❦

My intention throughout this book has been to remind you that no matter what you face, the Healer—Jesus—is available to hear your petitions and cries for mercy and help.

Jesus is close by when you feel hopeless or are brokenhearted. The Word of God is filled with examples of a loving, caring, and compassionate Father available to His children. His great compassion is a result of His great love for us.

Some people may question why there are diseases in the world if God is so loving and compassionate. Others struggle with seeing children who are sick and suffering before they even begin to live their lives. The devastations we see around us are not by God's design, and He is not the author of sickness or disease. Sickness and suffering result from the enemy's work in our world and the lives of people who live in the world.

Some people may ask why God allows it. The simple answer is that God gives us free will, and we choose to sin. By our choices, I mean that Adam and Eve gave in to the devil in the Garden of Eden and ate the fruit God told them not to eat. As a result of choosing to eat what God told them not to, sin and its consequences were birthed into the human race.

I have heard people say since God is such a big God, He could have stopped them. Maybe He could have, but then they would not have had the freedom of choice. They were given free will at birth, just as we were. We get to choose if we will eat, drink, smoke, or put things into our bodies that may cause us to be susceptible to sickness and disease. I am aware that many sicknesses and diseases are not always a result of what we have done, and the enemy brings some on. However, it has been proven that many things we ingest into our bodies are harmful to our lives.

Many wish they had made better life choices that did not adversely affect their health. I have a close friend whose mother smoked. When told about the harmful effects of smoking, she responded, "We all have to die from something." Unfortunately, she died from lung cancer a few years after making that statement. Cigarettes' harmful and toxic nature caused her to become ill and die prematurely. I do not believe we all have to die from something. I think we can live to a ripe old age, and after completing God's assignment for us on earth, we go home to be with Him. The Bible says healing is the children's bread (Matthew 15:26). It is God's antidote for Satan's actions in people's bodies. Jesus nailed sickness and disease to the cross at Calvary, and we were healed by His stripes (Isaiah 53:5).

Years ago, a song encouraged us to rise and be healed in the name of Jesus. The words to the song remind us there is healing in the name of Jesus. If, by faith, we ask the Father for healing in the name of Jesus, then according to His Word, we will have what we say.

This does not mean healing is always instantaneous. There are times when we have to wait for the manifestations. At other times, God may give us an instant miracle. If God does not heal you immediately, do not allow doubt to enter your heart. Jesus truly paid it all for us, but we must, by faith, do our part and accept the healing He provides.

In Mark 5, we read how Jesus delivered a demon-possessed man. When everyone saw the man clothed, and in his right mind, they were afraid. Instead of rejoicing with him, they told Jesus to leave. I believe they were afraid of the power that was displayed in the life of Jesus. Instead of desiring to know Him better, fear caused them to miss out on the healing and miracles they could have enjoyed in their lives.

After Jesus departed from this area, a group met Him when His ship docked. A Ruler of the Synagogue was among those who met Jesus and fell at His feet. The more time I spend studying the Word, the more I find that people amid their struggles will come and fall at the feet of Jesus. I believe this is important to note. When people find themselves in desperate situations, the most automatic response is to seek the One who has the solutions to their problems. Many in the Bible recognized they were in the presence of the Healer and chose to humble themselves before Him. When we operate in humility, we will always encounter the power of Jesus. As we acknowledge our limited abilities, we will recognize our God's sufficiency.

The Ruler of the Synagogue who met Jesus was an exalted leader of his time. He read and taught the Old Testament in the Jewish synagogue. These days we would call him a Pastor. He served as one of the overseers who took care of community problems, and legal transactions, officiated at funerals, and provided oversight for the synagogue. This man was also responsible for assigning the person who would bring the sermons each Sabbath. In those days, the people shared the messages, unlike today, where there is generally one pastor who delivers the message. I am painting a picture of who this man was so you clearly understand that this very prominent man recognized his need for the Savior's help. He humbled himself, falling at the feet of Jesus in plain view of the people who knew him, regardless of his high-ranking role in society. He was not ashamed to worship the One who had the solution to his problem.

His humility was because his daughter was at the point of death, and he wanted Jesus to heal her. His great need drove him to Jesus. He knew the laws and understood the scriptures but had not yet met the Healer of the Old and the New Testaments. Reading the scriptures will remind you Jesus is always at work in many people's lives.

When Jesus had crossed over again by boat to the other side, a large crowd gathered around Him while He was by the sea. One of the synagogue leaders, named Jairus, came, and when he saw Jesus, he fell at His feet and kept begging Him, "My little daughter is at death's door. Come and lay Your hands on her so she can get well and live." So Jesus went with him, and a large crowd was following and pressing against Him. A woman suffering from bleeding for twelve years had endured much under many doctors. She had spent everything she had and was not helped at all. On the contrary, she became worse. Having heard about Jesus, she came behind in the crowd and touched His robe. For she said, "If I can just touch His robes, I'll be made well!" Instantly the flow of blood ceased, and she sensed in her body that she was cured of her affliction.
Mark 5:21-29 (HCSB)

One significant thing to see in the scripture is this ruler begged Jesus for help. There is no shame in begging Jesus to heal or help you. Unlike most people around us, He has great compassion and will not mock or scorn us for needing Him. After Jesus responded to Jairus and began the journey to his home, a woman interrupted Him. Remember that Jairus' daughter was at the point of death, yet, Jesus stopped when the woman with the issue of blood touched Him. Along the journey of life, there will be many interruptions before receiving your miracle. Let's look closely at this woman's unwavering faith and her miracle.

The Interruption

At times as we pursue the miracles God has for us, we will encounter seasons when we are interrupted. Something in our lives will break our focus and cause us some delays. As important as our miracles are, we must understand that if God allows the interruption, it is for a more significant benefit in our lives or someone else's life.

The nameless woman with the issue of blood is a prime example of God showing us that interruptions are not always bad. Consider that she had been struggling for twelve years and could not get help from anyone, including the physicians. The Bible says life is in the blood (Leviticus 17:11); therefore, she had to be extremely weak with her blood loss over the twelve years. Her story speaks of perseverance and tenacious faith. This woman had heard about Jesus and the miracles He performed, so God dropped an unusual idea into her heart. This was God's special provision for His daughter, who had struggled for so long and endured so much.

She had to receive the word God spoke to her, believe it, and then move out in faith in what she heard. God told her to do something radical that had never been done before. She believed she was hearing from Him and embraced something totally outside the box, outside the norm, and outside what was legal and allowed. She was committed to what God said and believed that touching the hem of Jesus' garment would produce the desperately needed miracle. It did not matter; she had no example of this having ever been done before, this was her chance at freedom, and she grabbed it with all her might.

We must look at her journey to Jesus. The first thing we need to see about this time is people were considered unclean and had to stay away from the public if they had any type of blood disease. Therefore, I am convinced she probably told no one what God had instructed her to do to avoid anyone talking her out of taking this leap of faith. She also did not ask anyone for assistance because she probably could not trust them to keep her secret. God was her only help as she went to connect with Jesus.

As we study the life and ministry of Jesus, we find many people surrounding him wherever He went. This woman had to make her way through the crowd somehow to touch Him. Remember, she had been losing blood for years and was probably very weak. However, her condition did not stop her from pressing forward. She discovered where Jesus was to make His next appearance, and she made her way to connect with Him. When she arrived, Jesus was surrounded by the disciples plus His followers. To get to the hem of Jesus' garment required her to do something radical. In her weakened condition, she probably had to get down on the ground because it was impossible to reach the hem of His robe standing upright. Consider also that many people during that century wore robes, so she had to find and touch the right one to receive her miracle.

Imagine with me what this was like for this woman. She was sick with failing strength, yet she got down on the ground and crawled on her hands and knees to get to Jesus. I believe this was a test of her determination. How determined was she to receive her miracle? Would these obstacles keep her from moving forward? We often do not persevere as hard or as long as necessary to receive our miracle, but this woman did. As soon as she touched Jesus, power flowed out of Him, and she was healed.

Feeling the power leave His body, Jesus stopped and asked

who touched Him. The disciples showed their amazement at the question. How could Jesus ask who touched Him when the people surrounded Him? They did not know that this touch was not the typical touch of curiosity; it was a touch of great faith that pulled power out of Jesus. Fearful and trembling, the woman, probably still on her knees in the dust, spoke up. The entire crowd heard her testimony, and some were perhaps appalled she had ventured out in public with a blood condition.

Jesus, however, praised her for her unwavering faith, her act of obedience, her ability to hear the still, small voice of the Holy Spirit of God, and her fearless pursuit. This act secured her a place in Bible history while giving us an example of what Jesus can do with anyone who shows dogged faith to receive their miracle.

When Jesus addressed her, He called her daughter. You can hear the Father addressing His precious daughter, who had suffered for a long time. The Father had watched her many struggles and was moved with compassion for her. Jesus told her that her faith had made her whole. Being made whole means she was complete, unbroken, undestroyed, undiminished, and entire, lacking nothing in her life any longer.

The plan of the enemy to destroy her was unsuccessful. God the Father had taken the ashes of her life and given her beauty instead. He not only defeated the enemy on her behalf, but He also repaired everything that was previously destroyed in her life. Her miracle caused her to be noticed and pointed people toward Jesus.

Your faith will produce the same results for you. Miracles will always point people to Jesus. Jesus is never too busy for you to interrupt Him, so you can also receive your miracle. He is simply waiting for you to take a leap of faith, believing He is as available to you as He was to this woman. This miracle was not a random act but a part of God's grand plan to touch, change, and heal His daughter.

Some may feel your miracle has been interrupted because it has not yet come, and you think it was snatched away from you by the enemy. Often while waiting, we are left broken, frustrated, and hopeless. These feelings can cause us to be unproductive and make us unwilling to keep pressing onward. If we are not careful, we can become bitter because the outcome is not what we hoped it would be.

Jairus found himself in this situation. The miracle was just within his reach and was snatched away when this woman interrupted Jesus. He did not yet understand the Miracle Giver had resurrection power in His hands and could give him a greater miracle. God is faithful in that He will not allow the enemy to rob you of what He has planned to deposit into your life. The devil is a thief, but God will rescue and redeem what was stolen and give it back to you.

This unnamed woman is a hero, and her lesson is valuable for each of us. I believe when God does not tell us the name of a person in the Bible, you and I can put our names in the scripture and know that what He has done for them, He will also do for us.

Before this interruption, Jesus was heading to Jairus' home because his daughter was at the point of death. Therefore, can you imagine what was going through Jairus' mind? They were probably the same feelings and emotions you would have struggled with as Jesus delayed talking to this woman who was not dying, even though she had been desperately ill. Jairus' child was at death's door, yet Jesus was not in a hurry to get to her.

Jairus was probably anxious, nervous, impatient, frustrated, and even a little angry that Jesus was wasting time talking to this woman. Like many of us, he might have thought, "Come on, Jesus, You can deal with her issues later. My need is greater than hers."

Put yourself in Jairus' shoes. You probably would be wringing your hands and clenching your jaws to keep from screaming for

Jesus to get moving. Jairus was perhaps hoping, wishing, and desperately praying that Jesus would hurry up. Since the woman was already healed, there was no need for further conversation. Yet, Jesus talked with her. There was something else at work in the midst of this situation. Jairus' faith would require a level of belief beyond what was expected. Jesus was not only assigned to heal his daughter but also to raise her from the dead, so God's power would be demonstrated in a more significant way to all those who were following Him.

The Negative Report

The Bible says while Jesus was still speaking to the woman, the report came, "Jairus, your daughter is dead; why bother the teacher anymore?" This was a devastating and unwelcome report. Jesus, hearing the news, turned to Jairus and told him not to be afraid but just to believe. Believe what? Believe that the miracle could still be his? Believe his words when he first asked Jesus to heal his daughter?

Jesus was not surprised by the report and expected it to come. I believe the delay was intentional and planned by God because a greater revelation of who Jesus was and the power at His disposal would unfold among the people.

The first thing Jesus addressed when He spoke to Jairus was fear. This is one of the greatest weapons the devil uses against people. Jesus essentially told Jairus, "Don't let fear cause you to believe the wrong report." The report that his daughter was dead was a fact but not the final word.

Some of you have heard reports from the doctor and have had to choose whose report you will believe. Will you believe their report, though it appears to be accurate, or will you believe Jesus, who is Truth, has better information for your situation? His report is you are healed, cured, delivered, and set free. He says He is for you; therefore, you have all you need to be healed in the name of Jesus.

Jesus, the Truth, spoke to Jairus, and He told him only to believe. He said, "Do not do anything else, and just believe the report you have received is not the right report and what I plan to do will be the real deal."

Jesus reassured Jairus, and He does the same for us. He tells us not to let worry and anxiety settle in our hearts because we have the answer right in our midst, and He is the answer!

Jairus had to keep the same attitude of faith he had when he initially approached Jesus. He had to continue in faith that Jesus could still help his daughter. He was challenged not to let the adverse circumstances change his belief.

This is our challenge as well. The negative things we see can cause us to believe that Jesus will not help us. The negative reports are designed to cause us to change our minds. Jesus wants us to keep having faith in Him. We can trust Him for the right outcome. We must be convinced He will come through no matter what it looks like in the natural.

Jairus had to do only one thing in his situation, BELIEVE! The word 'only' means to solely, singly, merely, exclusively—just believe. He had to have one single focus—BELIEVE JESUS.

Like many of us, Jairus has been taught that death is final. Yet, Jesus asked him to believe something that seemed entirely impossible. It was impossible for man but not for Jesus. Since Jairus chose to believe, Jesus continued their journey. I am convinced had he decided not to believe, there would have been no further need for Jesus to journey home with him.

The Doubters

It is unfortunate, but there will always be some doubters when you begin to pursue Jesus for your miracle. Jesus gives us clear lessons in this story concerning what to do about those who doubt His ability to produce miracles in our lives.

He did not let anyone follow him except Peter, James and John the brother of James. When they came to the synagogue leader's home, Jesus saw a commotion, with people crying and wailing loudly. He went in and said to them, "Why all this commotion and wailing? The child is not dead but asleep." But they laughed at him. After he put them all out, he took the child's father and mother and the disciples who were with him, and went in where the child was.
Mark 5:37-40 (NIV)

Jesus tightened His circle before performing this miracle, and we should follow His example. We first see He did not take all twelve disciples with Him. The crowds of spectators who had followed Him were not allowed to continue their journey either. He only took three of the disciples, the ones closest to Him, and the other nine disciples were left to await His return.

I hope, like me, many of you desire an invitation to go with Jesus when He begins to work in the lives of others. This requires we develop a close and intimate relationship with Him so He never feels the need to exclude us from the miracles He is about to perform because we might be unprepared.

Jesus was fully aware that when He arrived at the house, there would be spectators and unbelievers, so there was no need to take others with Him. The people were causing such a commotion Jesus questioned them about it. Jesus told them the child was not dead but sleeping, and they laughed and mocked Him. What was Jesus telling them? He told them the time that the child was dead was as if she had been only sleeping for a short time. He tried to reassure them she would not remain in that state for long, but they did not have the faith of Jairus.

Understand when Jesus, the Resurrection, and the Life, show up, anything that has experienced a premature death will not remain dead. The people continued to laugh and mock Him, so He put them out of the house and closed the door. I must pause here and address this. You and I must recognize those in our midst who are not on the Lord's side. Not every person who says they believe really believes in the miracle-working power of Jesus. We must be careful not to allow doubters and unbelievers in when we desperately need a miracle. Their lack of faith and scoffing can either delay the miracle or cause us to question whether God can deliver His Word. These people can cause us to doubt and waver. Jesus shows us what we must do to ensure we receive our miracle:

- *Separate ourselves from the doubters and unbelievers.*
- *Shut our ears to their laughter and mocking.*
- *Do not entertain them.*
- *Put them out of our midst.*
- *Do not allow them in our inner circle.*
- *Recognize those not on board with us and stop sharing the nuggets God gives us.*

After Jesus closed the door, He tightened the circle even more. He only took the three disciples, the mother, and the father, with Him. They would be the first eyewitnesses to this amazing miracle. What excellent training and equipping this was for the disciples as they prepared to spread the gospel to the world. Remember, every miracle is designed to draw unbelievers closer to God.

Daughter, Arise

Jesus set the stage for this creative miracle. If you were on the outside, I am sure you would be wondering what He would do and if it was possible to raise a person from the dead. The doubt and unbelief were probably palatable. If you were a part of the inner circle, the anticipation and the excitement must have been intense and unbearable. The disciples and Jairus had just witnessed the healing of a woman who simply touched His garment. Now they were about to experience something more significant than what had previously occurred. They probably had some uncertainty about whether it was possible. Mark 10:27 tells us it may be impossible with men, but it is possible with God. Let's read what Jesus did to the girl.

He took her by the hand and said to her, "Talitha koum!" (which means, "Little girl, I say to you, get up!"). Immediately the girl stood up and began to walk around (she was twelve years old). At this, they were completely astonished. He gave strict order not to let anyone know about this and told them to give her something to eat.
Mark 5:41-43 (NIV)

Even as I type this scripture, I can feel the power and authority of Jesus, and I am in awe He has given us this same authority to heal the sick and raise the dead. I desire to walk in His shoes, and I hope that is your desire. In Luke 7, when He raised the widow's son, Jesus simply said, 'Arise.' In John 11, when He raised Lazarus, He told him to come forth. Jesus simply told them to wake up and begin again. He gave them a brand new start. He raised them from an untimely death because it was not their time and because God wanted to demonstrate His authority over death and the grave. In raising them, Jesus gave hope and healing to the families who were grieving. God does everything to heal and help us because He loves us completely.

As soon as Jesus spoke the words, without hesitation, the young girl got up and walked. 2 Corinthian 5:8 tells us to be absent from the body is to be present with the Lord. At the moment Jesus told her to arise, her spirit, which had gone back to God from whence it came, instantly returned to her body, and she experienced resurrection life. The scripture says they were astonished. Who was astonished? The disciples had walked closely with Him and the young girl's parents. It is one thing for the parents to be surprised, but the disciples should have known by now the incredible power of Jesus. Yet, they also were amazed.

Jesus told them not to tell anyone what had happened. How was this possible, seeing the girl was alive? It was very evident He did something to cause her to live. Let me propose something— could He have told them not to share how the miracle took place? How easy it was? He had not prayed, pleaded, or begged God for help. Jesus simply acted on what He knew about His Father. God had the power to raise the dead and assigned Jesus as His instrument to accomplish this. He did what He told Jairus to do, ONLY BELIEVE! They were surprised, amazed, astounded, and stood in awe and wonder at God's power that was displayed in the life of Jesus.

It is interesting to note they had doubted He could raise the girl, which is why they were so astonished. This miracle was a training exercise in BELIEVING and a reminder that the disciples were connected to the Source of Life Himself. Jesus understood His power and authority, and He simply operated in it. He desires we do the same.

What needs to be raised in your life? Is it your health? What about a dead relationship? Do you need to see a resurrection of your purpose and vision? What about your level of authority?

This same Jesus, with all power and authority in His hands, has given it to you. The Power who raised Him from the dead is available to you. He lives in you and will give you the same ability to be used by God the Father. He is the Holy Spirit whom Jesus sent to live in every believer. He has given us the ability to speak to the dead things in our lives and experience God's resurrection power in our midst.

All you need to do is ONLY BELIEVE! Use your authority and command health to spring forth, body to be healed, broken relationships to be restored, finances to be fixed, and God to be glorified in your life. Since God has given you the same authority He gave His Son, there is no reason to doubt He will answer you and give you the same results He gave Jesus. He loves you and wants you to be healed and made whole in all areas of your life. Rise and be healed in the name of Jesus.

Lessons To Live By

- In your need, fall at the feet of Jesus.
- Even though there are interruptions in your life, your miracle will still happen.
- Don't get impatient while waiting for Jesus to act.
- Don't let frustration impede you.
- Operate in faith and not in fear.
- Keep the same attitude of faith you had when you initially approached Jesus.
- Remove the doubters and unbelievers from your midst.
- Believe only the report of Jesus.
- Go into the inner court with Jesus so you can witness great and wonderful things.
- When the situations seem dead, ONLY BELIEVE.

A Scripture For Healing – John 6:63

Father, I thank You that You said in John 6:63 that the Holy Spirit gives life and that the words You have spoken over me are full of the Spirit and are pregnant with life. Thank You that as I take Your Word into my heart, it will spring forth and bear the right fruit in my life. Thank You for providing a way to escape from all of my emotional, physical, and spiritual struggles. In Jesus' name. Amen!

Are You My Healer?

⁓⁓⁓

The Bible says Jesus is the same yesterday, today, and forever (Hebrews 13:8). This is a reminder He can and will do whatever He has done in the past. When we recognize how powerful Jesus is and the power available to us because the Holy Spirit lives in us, we will be unstoppable as it relates to seeing people healed, delivered, and set free by the power of God.

On one of our mission trips overseas, we witnessed the power of God in action in a hospital filled with sick children.

It is always the practice of the ministry to visit hospitals and pray for the sick on every mission trip we take. God wants to heal the sick! On this trip, we had taken a lot of gifts for the children in the hospital, but due to a problem with customs not wanting to release our van, which contained all the goods, we could not take the items to the children when we first visited.

The day we arrived at the hospital was a very busy one for them. The first floor, which was the children's wing, was filled to overflowing with sick children. All the rooms housed eight to ten beds each and were filled. Children were on beds in the hallways and even close to the elevators. The sight was overwhelming. After dividing the team into groups, we began to pray and lay hands on the sick as instructed in Mark 16:18. After several hours of praying, we left the hospital.

As we approached our van, I heard the Lord say He would heal every child and send them home within a week. As an act of faith, I told the team what God said, and we agreed in prayer He would do it. I believe God has the power to empty every hospital in the world of sick people, and I pray this continually. One week later, customs finally released our goods, and we returned to the hospital to give the children their gifts.

I wondered if we were at the right place when we walked in. The halls were empty, and so were ninety-five percent of the rooms. Each team went to the area where they had previously prayed for the kids, and in amazement, we came back together in the hall because there were no children in the rooms. Down the hall, I spotted a doctor and asked where the children who had been in the hospital the previous Friday were. He told us they all went home during the week, and only two remained from the last Friday, and they were also ready to be released. We were stunned! God had done what He said He would do, and we were shocked. Oh, ye of little faith. The doctor told us there were a few new patients, so we prayed for them and gave them and the hospital staff the gifts we had brought. To answer the question, "God is indeed our healer."

The miracle Jesus did in the hospital has been a road map for me concerning how He wants to heal and set people free. The emotional pain that comes with the burden of sickness, especially in countries where people cannot afford to go to the doctor, can be unbearable. Not only do we pray for the children, but we also minister and pray for the family members. I believe we often see more healings and miracles overseas because the people only have God to rely on. They genuinely put their faith in Him as their healer. Remember, I told you He is our great Physician, and repeatedly, He has proven this to us.

As you read Matthew, Mark, Luke, and John, you will experience the healing power of God through Jesus as He walked on earth. John 14:12 tells us we will do greater works because He is going to the Father. For many years, I have wondered and also asked the question of how we can do greater works than Jesus. He healed the sick, cleansed the leper, delivered the demon-possessed, and raised the dead. I have come to a few conclusions, which I will share with you.

We have the same resurrection power of the Holy Spirit living in us. He is the same Power that raised Jesus from the dead; therefore, we are equipped with all we need to do the work He did. In addition, while Jesus was here, He did not have the benefits of television, radio, e-mails, text, etc., available today to spread the good news. Jesus walked or rode a donkey wherever He traveled; therefore, He could not cover a vast territory. Today, we have many forms of transportation that enable us to take the gospel to many unreached people groups worldwide. As of the writing of this book, the current statistic is that there are approximately seventy-two thousand unreached groups (2.87 billion people) in the world who need to hear the gospel of our Lord Jesus Christ. In Matthew 24:14, Jesus told us He would return when the gospel has been shared with all people. We have been given the tools to reach the world, and more significant work has begun. It is our responsibility to ask God how He can use us to effect change in the lives of the people in our communities and worldwide. We must desire to obey and follow the example of Jesus.

One of the things I love about Jesus is His compassion as He dealt with those in various life struggles. He is compassionate and caring whether our struggles are emotional, physical, or relational. Wherever you are in your life, He will come in and rescue you. Over the years, I have had the privilege to minister to people who were sick in their bodies and to see some incredible miracles. At other times, I have ministered to people with emotional and mental struggles who also experienced the healing power of the Savior. In this chapter, I want to share some of the most wonderful emotional, mental, and physical miracles I have witnessed as I answer the question, "Are You, my Healer?"

Freedom For the Oppressed

When I am not teaching a message or running the ministries' day-to-day functions, I often counsel people or minister one-on-one with those going through a rough patch. Using a program called Sozo, I have often closed doors in people's lives that they might have opened to the enemy. Sometimes, people open doors to the enemy and may not be fully aware of what they have done. But there are other times when people open some dangerous spiritual doors because they think obtaining more knowledge is fun. As a result of these decisions, we have taken many people through inner healing deliverance sessions. I have seen the kindness and love of God on display as He sets people free.

In a deliverance session, I met a young girl in a deep mental and emotional struggle. She opened the door to the enemy, not realizing she was walking into a trap designed for her downfall. She and a friend were invited by a stranger to get their palms read. She walked into the session and came out completely changed. Before this encounter, I understood that she was brilliant, had good grades, and was already taking college courses. Once she went through the session, she came away not remembering what had happened and could not function like the ordinary eighteen-year-old girl she had been. She spent many days in the hospital and lost a tremendous amount of weight. In addition, she began to act as if she was about ten years old and could not continue with school. She needed assistance from her family just to function daily.

When she came into the deliverance session, she could not articulate what had happened to her, so it was difficult to get to the root of what doors had been opened to the enemy. Relying solely on the power of the Holy Spirit for guidance, my team and I prayed and began to take her through some prayers designed to set her free. I am incredibly grateful to the Lord for His wisdom as He led us step-by-step through the many doors the enemy had used to gain access to her life. After much praying, I commanded the spirits to get out and to go where Jesus sends them (Luke 8:31). Then I had her pray using the authority Jesus gave her to renounce the devil and to evict his evil spirits from her life. Operating in the power and authority, we have in the name of Jesus, we did battle for her freedom. I will be the first to admit the condition she was in seemed hopeless, and I was unsure what the result would be even though I understood what Jesus could do. We finished the session a few hours later, and her mom took her home.

A few months later, I revisited the city to minister at a church. During the greeting, this beautiful young woman came and hugged me. I would not have recognized her if her mom had not stood directly behind her. Jesus healed her! She was alert, vibrantly alive, and fully aware of who she was and where she was. The deadness in her eyes was replaced with the brilliant light of Jesus shining through her. Amazing! After the service, I heard the result of God's transforming work over the previous months. She was back in school and preparing to graduate with high grades. She was also preparing to go to nursing school. God did what only He could do. He went into the dark recesses of her mind and set her free from the enslavement of the enemy. She was emotionally lost and mentally incapable of functioning, but God set her completely free. What an awesome God we serve. Even now, I am still amazed by His transforming power.

Is He Your Healer? Your resounding answer should be YES. Think about the emotional baggage He has delivered you from and remind yourself if He has done it before, He will do it again. Many of you can share testimonies of how God came into your darkness and brought the light of His glory into your heart. When no one could rescue you, He did. When the situation seemed hopeless, Jesus showed you nothing is hopeless to those who are connected to Him. Some of you thought you would experience fear forever, but He has erased the pain of the past and given you a new lease on life. I am reminded of two scriptures. John 8:36 tells us whom the Son sets free is free indeed, and 2 Corinthians 5:17 says, "Therefore if any man be in Christ, he is a new creature: old things are passed away; behold, all things become new." You are a new person because He has wiped the slate clean and given you a fresh start. Do not allow your past associations or the devil to entangle you again in bondage.

My team and I have seen God's miracle working power at work in many lives. We have also encountered the enemy's stronghold as God begins to set His people free. In another deliverance session, we discovered the enemy could be tenacious in his grip on a person's mind. As we prayed and sought the Lord for deliverance for the person in this particular session, the enemy told us he would wear us out because he was not leaving. He said he had been given permission to enter this person's life, and we were not evicting him. It took a while, but with the help of the Holy Spirit and Jesus, he was expelled and sent packing.

In another session, right before we concluded, the person leading the deliverance felt other spirits, who did not want to be identified, were hiding within the person. She asked us to pray for wisdom and guidance. As we prayed, God gave us the answer. When she called out the deaf and dumb spirits, the individual whose head was hanging down looked up instantly with a surprised look on her face. The look said, "How did you know?"

The spirits were shocked they had been discovered. Our team leader responded the Lord will always reveal the enemy and faithfully set His children free.

The emotional battles we face are often traumatic and devastating. They can cause us to limp through life because, often, they are not addressed by those closest to us. In these sessions, I have found numerous people who experienced horrible things in their childhood that left them with heavy emotional baggage. Many people have not experienced the healing they need because they had no one to share their struggles and hurts with, so they continued to carry them daily and even for years.

Jesus died to free us not only from physical struggles but also from emotional wounds as well. He has provided a way of escape, and we must seek Him to receive our healing. As crucial as healing is for our bodies, it is equally, if not more important, that we are healed in our minds and emotions. If we do not experience healing in those areas, we can sabotage our physical healing by what we think and speak over ourselves.

Hospice To Healing

I cannot conclude this book without sharing an amazing miracle Jesus performed for a lady who would have died without His intervention. I was ministering in a city in Texas, and right after the first service, I was asked to pray for a lady who was having difficulty breathing and could not stand for long periods. When I approached her, I realized she was one of the church's faithful members who had been recently diagnosed with cancer. The doctor told her she had developed advanced cancer due to asbestos. As I laid my hands on her and prayed for her, the Lord whispered Psalm 118:17 into my ears. It says, "I shall not die, but live, and declare the works of the Lord."

The following month I was again ministering in the same city. The woman was unable to attend because she had deteriorated quickly. The doctors felt chemotherapy would not help her condition, so they gave her no hope. After the service, we went to her home to pray with her. As I stepped out of the car, the Holy Spirit prompted me to take the Bible and to find and pray every healing scripture over her I could recall. We took her Bible and highlighted the scriptures, putting her name into each healing promise. My intention was she could read and pray the words over herself. As I prepared to hand her the Bible, the Holy Spirit said, "She does not have the strength to hold the Bible. Find her a healing CD so she can listen to the Word."

We went to the store but could not find a healing CD. I strongly felt God did not want me to leave the city without giving it to her. So I asked Him what I should do since I could not find one. His answer was simple, "Record one." It is incredible how simple and straightforward the Holy Spirit is when He instructs us. Before He said that it had never dawned on me to make the CD.

I found sixty healing promises in the Word, recorded the scriptures, and had music added to it. As I finalized this, the Holy Spirit reminded me of another lady with lupus who had been in the hospital for several weeks. He told me to send her a CD. Within a week of listening to the CD, this lady was released from the hospital and doing better.

A few months passed, and I was again in the city. The lady with cancer came to the service, but she was now in a wheelchair. She had lost a significant amount of weight and was extremely frail and unable to perform even her basic needs. Again, I prayed with her, and God reiterated Psalm 118:17.

A few weeks after this trip, I received a call that her condition had deteriorated further, and the doctor recommended she be placed in hospice for her last days. I got mad at the devil! I prayed and reminded God of the promises in His Word and the promises He had given to her. I also reminded Him how devastated her family and church family would be if she died. Her church, her family, and my team had rallied around her and constantly prayed for God's intervention. I refused to accept she would die because God is not a man, and He cannot lie. What He has promised, He is faithful to perform (Numbers 23:19-20). I also refused to give myself a way out. At times, we will attempt to give ourselves a way out when we do not receive the things for which we are standing in faith. We make statements like these, "Maybe I did not hear God. Maybe I missed it. Maybe I gave her false hope." When things do not work out as we hope, some people will find reasons and excuses for why it did not happen. I believed I heard God, and I made a demand on the promises in His Word. God does not need us to make excuses for Him or to justify why He did not perform our miracles. He will do what He says. If the outcome is different from what we believe, then we must understand His ways are far above ours and trust His decision.

In prayer, I declared she would not need to go into the hospice, and God would heal and deliver her. After a month, I received no further word about the hospice, so I continued to believe God. I was in the same city a month later to minister. The first night I was at the church, out walked this lady, and she was moving fast. She was out of the wheelchair and was gloriously healed by the power of Jesus! This stopped me in my tracks, and in total amazement, I called her name. I could not believe what I saw. Seeing the demonstration of God's power and faithfulness, my team and I were overcome with joy. The church members had not updated me on her recovery because they wanted me to see the results myself. I was so glad because I had to see it for myself.

When I left the city, the lady was out bowling with her Home Group and enjoying life. God continues to finalize her healing.

God is our healer! We do not often understand who and when He will heal, so we must trust and obey His Word until we see the results. I cannot express my awe of God's amazing grace and power. I pray you will also experience His miracles and wonders in profound ways in your life.

Retaining Your Healing

After His resurrection and just before Jesus left earth and returned to heaven, He gave the disciples a commission in the book of Mark.

> *He said, "Go into all the world and preach the gospel to the whole creation. Whoever believes and is baptized will be saved, but whoever does not believe will be condemned. And these signs will accompany those who believe: In My name they will drive out demons; they will speak in new languages; they will pick up snakes; if they should drink anything deadly, it will never harm them; they will lay hands on sick and they will get well.*
> *Mark 16:15-18 (HCSB)*

In this scripture, there is an important message Jesus taught that I believe is one of the greatest keys for a person to hold on to their healing and freedom in Christ. The first thing we see in the commission is He told the disciples to *drive out demons*. I believe this is significant because if the demonic spirits are not driven out, people cannot hold on to their healing. The demonic spirits have to be driven out in the name of Jesus so that people can experience freedom from the grip of the enemy and his habitual torment of their minds and emotions. We are often plagued in our minds with various scenarios of what could be wrong in our bodies before we have any symptoms. Our minds will project the false images of the devil's lies to us before they ever manifest in the natural. Satan's grip on our minds can be so deep-seated we have to fight hard to free ourselves. Jesus tells us if we cast him out and break his grip, we will be able to hold on to the freedom He gives us.

Think about the things that have controlled your life. Can you see that many of those things first occurred in your mind? The thoughts were so harassing that you eventually began to believe them and act as if they were real. The wounds in our hearts and the hurts from the past leave the same impression of not being able to get free from the things that bind us. Jesus wants you to know that freedom is available through the power of the Holy Spirit, who lives in your heart.

Over the years, I have come to see something clearly. As wonderful as modern medicine is and as helpful as doctors are at easing our physical pain, they cannot heal the body. What doctors do is cut away the disease so that healthier tissues can grow. They can remove the cancerous cells and the damaged tissues, but they cannot mend the body—only God can. Once they have surgery, they stitch us up and send us home to heal. They cannot aid in the healing process but can give us medicine to help us with the pain while we recover. God mends the broken tissues and heals the wounds over time. Our great Physician is the only one who can cause new tissues to develop and grow in our bodies.

The same applies to our emotional scars. Only God can heal them, and He has the power to go into the broken places in our hearts and clean up the messes that have become embedded in our souls. We may never know how He does it, but many of us have experienced freedom from emotional traumas.

I am constantly reminded of how much we need God. Without Him, life would be unbearable. As I conclude this book, I invite you to ask yourself if He is your healer and then answer the question. Reflect on the many places in your life where God has brought His healing power. Remember how wounded, afraid, and alone you have been at various times, and then see how far you have come in the journey with God's help and healing.

Throughout this book, I have shared many biblical stories of lives that were touched, healed, and transformed by the power of Jesus and the healing touch of the Holy Spirit. In each story, you could see that God loved these people as He loves you, and you can claim any of those healings for yourself. The same God who healed, delivered, and set them free can and will do the same for you.

If you are wounded in your soul, ask Jesus to come and heal the wounds and give you a fresh start. He can provide you with a new lease on life. To experience this new life, you must let go of the things in your past that have left you scarred and broken. You must forgive the offenders so you can experience freedom. Forgiveness is not for offenders; it is for you, so you can be free of sorrow and bitterness, which are traps of the enemy.

I have shared this example for many years as I minister the Word. Have you ever had a scar on your body that appears to be healed? You were able to see the scar and recall how you got it. All seemed well over the years until someone said something or did something and inadvertently pressed against the scar, and to your dismay, you felt pain and discomfort from what you thought was healed.

Sometimes we do not deal with the root of the problem; we only address the symptoms. The root issue is still there, but the medication has nullified the symptoms and fooled us into believing healing has taken place. You and I will never experience the joy of being free if we do not dig up the root of the problem and deal with it layer by layer until we experience freedom.

I was recently inspired to pick up a plant that appeared to be dying on the surface and look closely to see if there was still life in it. I felt the prompting of the Holy Spirit to turn it over and look at the bottom of the pot. To my surprise, roots were growing in all directions, signifying that the plant was not dying and needed to be nourished.

Sometimes we believe our healing has not manifested because we will not look closely to see if it has occurred. Like the plant, it appears dead on the surface, but there is still life underneath. I challenge you not to cover up the issues in your life. Ask Jesus to help you dig up the painful roots and deal with them one by one, with the help of the Holy Spirit, until you are free indeed. Jesus wants you to be healed in all areas of your life so that He can showcase His life and His power through you. You must be a genuine reflection to the world that He is the only One who can heal you and make you whole.

Lessons To Live By

- Jesus has the power to heal and set you free.
- When Jesus speaks a word to your heart, choose to believe and embrace it.
- God is still the Miracle Worker, and He still works miracles today.
- For every wound in your life, there is a promise in the Word for your healing.
- The same Jesus who healed others will also heal you. He is no respecter of persons.
- Go after the roots of the problems in your life, and don't stop until they are entirely rooted out.
- Remember, there is power in the name of Jesus.
- Finally, God can heal you, and He is always available when you ask Him.

A Scripture For Healing – Isaiah 53:4-5

Father, in the name of Jesus, I thank You for Your promise in Isaiah that Jesus took my infirmities and carried my sorrows. I also thank You that He was pierced for my transgressions; He was crushed for my iniquities; the punishment that brought my peace was upon Him; and by His wounds, I am healed. Today, as an act of my will, I receive His sacrifice. I am determined to walk fully in my healing, in Jesus' name.
Amen!

Beloved!

Beloved, do you know how deep my thoughts are toward you? Above all things, I wish, hope, and desire that your life may be full to overflowing with good health. I want you to prosper in your body, emotions, soul, home, family, and every aspect of your life.

I am with you in your struggles. I have not ever taken my eyes off you. I have wept with you. I have held you in your pain and brokenness. I have comforted you in your sickness. I brought you hope when you were hopeless. The little things that happened to lift your spirit when you were worn out were sent from Me.

I am not the one who brought sickness, devastation, emotional wounds, or trouble to your life. They were sent by the evil one, the accuser of the brethren, to destroy you; however, I have caused you to prevail. I will turn what he meant for evil in your life into your finest, most triumphant moments.

Come to me all who are weary, hopeless, discouraged, distraught, broken, troubled, or ashamed, and I will give you rest. I do not burden you; I will lift the load from your shoulders and fill you with my peace.

Beloved, I am with you and will never leave or forsake you. You are my dearly loved one. You are the apple of my eye. You are fearfully and wonderfully made. I have engraved you on the palms of my hands, close to the scars I bore for you, and no one can pluck you out of my hands.

I love you, my beloved one. So, in your struggles, do not forget I am in it with you and will deliver you out of them all. This is my promise, and it is as sure as the dawn.

FROM THE FATHER'S HEART!

A Prayer for Salvation

Father, I acknowledge You sent Jesus into the world to die for my sins. I believe He is Your Son; He was born of a virgin, and He died and rose from the dead for my sins. I acknowledge I have sinned and fallen short of Your standards and ask You to forgive me. I invite Jesus to come into my heart because the Bible says He is the way, truth, and life, and no man comes to the Father but by Him. Father, I am coming to You in the precious name of Your Son, Jesus. I thank You for saving me and setting me free, in Jesus' name.

Amen! (So Be It).

Notes

1. Zondervan Bible Commentary
   FF Bruce, General Edition
   (Grand Rapids, MI)

2. Vine's Expository Dictionary
   Edited by Stephen D. Renn
   Hendrickson Publishers Marketing LLC

About the Author

Joan Murray is committed to helping people discover their destinies. She is the founder and CEO of Joan Murray Ministries and Seeds of Hope Worldwide Missions. Joan is dedicated to teaching, training, equipping, and helping people with various life struggles.

Joan is a minister, Bible teacher, author, and missionary. She has traveled extensively throughout the United States and internationally sharing the gospel message and serving the needs of the oppressed. Joan currently resides in Houston, Texas.

If you would like to know more about Joan Murray Ministries or Seeds of Hope Worldwide Missions, please get in touch with us at:

Joan Murray Ministries & Seeds Of Hope Worldwide Missions
26340 FM 1736
Waller, TX 77848
281-398-2501
email: jmmcontactus@gmail.com
website: www.jemmuniquegift.com
website: www.joanmurrayministries.org

Changing Lives Through the Power and Truth of God's Word.

facebook.com/jmmseedsofhope

x.com/@jmmseedsofhope

instagram.com/joan_murray_ministries

threads.net/@joan_murray_ministries

amazon.com/Lord-Make-Me-Whole-Healing/dp/B0BJYJNQX1

youtube.com/@JoanMurrayMinistries

linkedin.com/in/joan-e-murray-042aba17b

www.ingramcontent.com/pod-product-compliance
Lightning Source LLC
Chambersburg PA
CBHW071154120626
46546CB00006B/2254